The Official American Sign Language Writing Textbook

Written by
Robert Arnold Augustus,
Elsie Ritchie and Suzanne Stecker

Edited by
Elisa Abenchuchan Vita

http://aslized.org

http://si5s.org

This book is dedicated to
Dr. Lawrence "Larry" Fleischer
who paved the road for ASL literacy
during the recent times.

© 2013, ASLized and si5s

All rights reserved. No part of this book may be reproduced or transmitted in any form or by any means electronic, or mechanical, including photocopying, recording, or by any information storage or retrieval system, without written permission from ASLized and si5s.

Printed in the United States of America

ISBN: 978-1-4675-4293-7

The paper used in this publication is smooth gloss on 100# text and 100# cover using an offset printer. Layout was completed in Adobe InDesign CS6. Adobe Photoshop CS6 was relied to extract still images of the body, facial expressions, and handshapes from movie clips as originally produced in Autodesk Maya 3D. All vector-based illustrations were developed in Adobe Illustrator CS6.

Acknowledgments

We would love to thank our families and dear friends for their unconditional love as we spent countless hours working on "The Official American Sign Language Writing Textbook." We also want to recognize Etta Stecker, Suzanne's mother, for her encouragement during ASLized's early days. She rooted every vision we shared and we looked up to her with a great respect.

This is also an opportunity to extend our heartfelt gratitude to Robert Arnold Augustus, the inventor of ASL writing, for inviting us to co-author this textbook with him. Because of him, we are forever grateful to be able to read and write ASL now.

Finally, we would like to thank the whole ASL community for their faith and support as we create a new addition to ASL literacy. This textbook belongs to every signing individual, especially for the children of tomorrow.

—ASLized Team

Writing this piece of acknowledgments turned into an inspiring task. I did not realize how huge the community of friends and families over the years has collaborated, disagreed and reasoned in this pioneering process to make this writing system possible. The two books inspired me to make ASL writing possible: "Wittgenstein's Poker" by David Edmonds and John Eidinow; and "The Mad Man And The Professor" by Simon Winchester. After reading the books I had to do something about ASL.

My deep thank you to the following friends in making ASL writing possible: Dr. Randolph Mowry for giving your free time to getting this off the ground. Without your help I would not have been so inspired; Dr. H-Dirksen Bauman, Dr. Gene Mirus, Dr. Ben Bahan, Dr. Laura-Ann Pettito, and Florian Coulmas for your support in this writing system that should be necessary; Nicholas Zerlentes for your work with the business of this book; Suzanne Stecker and Elsie Ritchie of ASLized for jumping in at a moment's need to work with me and with belief in ASL writing, produce this book; and Dr. Lawrence Fleischer, for supporting me and seeing ASL writing as an important instrument in ASL literacy.

It is you the reader and the community that continue to build this system now in your hands. Thank you all my friends near and far for believing and not, and giving support, or remaining silent, in making ASL literacy possible.

—si5s Team

Contents

Introduction: About iv
    Essentials of ASL Written System v
    Sign Language and Terminology for the Written System vi
    Fundamentals of ASL Writing vii

Chapter One: Digibet 2
    Left and Right 3
    Dominant Digit: Left or Right 4
    Thumb Mark 4
    Sans Thumb Mark 4
    Front Locative Marks 5
    Side Locative Marks 5
    Digits 6

Chapter Two: Diacritic Marks and Endpoints 12
    Hinge 13
    Ring 14
    Flutter 14
    Pull 15
    Half Square 15
    Rattle 15
    Open 16
    Bar or Edge 16
    Double Bars 16
    Endpoints 17
    Verb, Noun and Action Endpoints 17
    One Motion 17
    Two Motions 17
    Three or More Motions 18
    Diacritic Marks with Endpoints 18

Chapter Three: Movement Line and Morphs 20
    Movement Line and Endpoint 21
    Directional Movement 22
    Patterned Movement 23

Chapter Three: Movement Line and Morphs (continued)

    Random Movement 23

    Other Motions 24

    Alternating Marks. 24

    Repeating Movement Lines and Endpoints. 25

    Palm Orientation and Movement Line Combination 26

    Motion Morphs 27

    Stationary Morphs 28

Chapter Four: Non-Manual Signals **30**

    Mouth. 31

    Eyebrow. 33

    Nose 33

Chapter Five: Reserved Marks **36**

    Pronouns 37

    Possessive Pronouns 38

    Verb 38

    Pause 39

    Person/People 39

    Time Indicator 40

Chapter Six: Composition **42**

    Digits 43

    Locative Marks. 43

    Non-Manual Signal Marks. 44

    Motion Line and Endpoint. 46

    Pause Marks. 46

Chapter Seven: Further Readings. **48**

    George Veditz: Preservation of ASL 49

    Joseph Davis: Deaf-Blind Ninja 50

    Ella Lentz: The Treasure. 51

Glossary. **58**

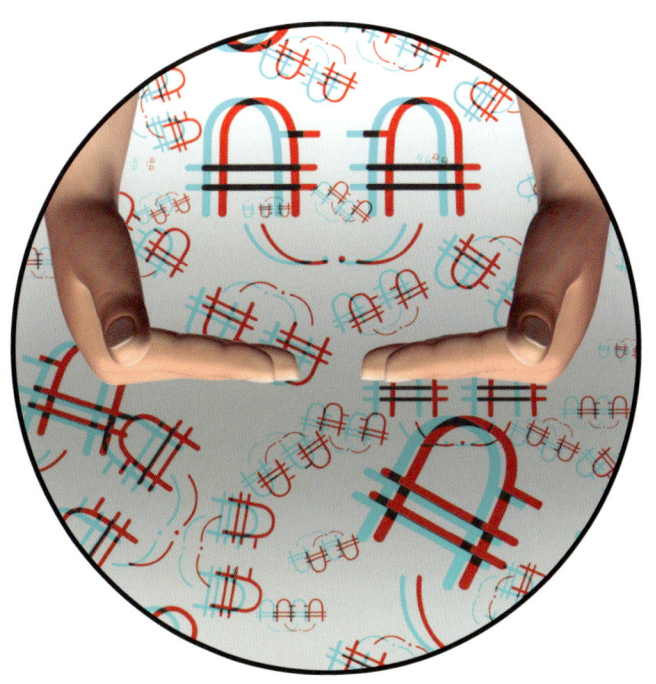

Introduction

About

The Official American Sign Language Writing Textbook aims to offer a new opportunity in the curriculum teaching of American Sign Language (ASL). Traditionally, ASL does not have a written form. ASL users have historically used English (or another written language, depending on where they live) to write down their thoughts, even though they communicate with each other using ASL.

Ideas can be, and are often, lost in translation. What are we losing when we translate our thoughts in ASL before writing them on paper in English? It is an unanswerable question, but an important one. This textbook puts forward a complete and practical written system that enables us to put ASL directly on the page.

Essentials of Written ASL System

All over the world, ASL is used and taught as a language with no written form. This does not make ASL unique, since a large percentage of languages spoken in the world today also do not have a written form. However, there are plenty of spoken languages that have a written form, such as English and Spanish, yet there is not a single **sign language** in the world that has a written form.

The written word, when published for people to read, carries with it a power to spread a message, to convey one's thoughts and emotions, and to inspire and/or provoke others. The world as it is today would not be here without the circulation of knowledge and the influence of literature if not for the pen, the typewriter, or the keyboard.

Why are the signed languages of our world, used and beloved by so many, missing this significant aspect of a language? There have been some efforts in the past, but this textbook proposes a more practical, visual approach to written ASL.

Written ASL will also offer the ASL community an opportunity to develop a **corpus** of written ASL, including literature, academic papers, and all kinds of text will stand as a formal record that presents to the world the unique perspective of those in the ASL community.

The ASL writing system will also be a way to document every aspect of the language, forming an effective map for those within and outside of the ASL community to travel through the land of ASL. All kinds of text, including literature, social messages, educational materials, and political discourse, will be available for all to read, to interpret, and to understand. Written text in ASL will enable everyone to gain access to the ASL world, even if they do not have an ASL native to guide them. Books, journals, literature, and textbooks in written ASL will offer a road map into the ASL community for all who wish to visit.

Written ASL will also benefit those who are raised with ASL as their first language. There has always been a missing link in the written language acquisition for native users of ASL, since they are forced to learn the writing system of their second language, e.g. English, without first mastering the writing system of their own native language. This gap between their L1, or first language, and their **second written language** have led to significant struggles and frustration for some ASL natives. They jump into the second language learning without their own written form as a reference point.

With the new writing system that is outlined in this textbook, ASL users now will have the opportunity to learn the written system of their native language and then apply that knowledge to their learning of a second language, be it English or any other written language. Written ASL will serve as a stepping-stone into the world of written languages for the ASL community.

Sign Language and Terminology for the Written System

The languages can be categorized into two groups: oral and manual languages, or vocal and sign languages. The oral and vocal languages have been recognized, studied, written, and given linguistic and **laymen's terms** for centuries.

However, only 50 years ago, William Stokoe brought ASL to the world stage and declared that it was a language in its own right.

Since then, **linguists** have placed ASL and other sign languages under the language umbrella and gave them manual language terminologies, both linguistic and layman.

Unfortunately, more often than not, the tools used to analyze sign languages have historically been the same as those that have been used to analyze oral languages. This is where the problem arises.

Even though both oral and manual languages have many characteristics in common, those of which all languages in the world must consist, they are also very different. Sign language uses **spatial orientation** and movement signals to convey messages, which are all elements that are not seen in most oral languages.

Rather than analyzing sign languages as the oranges that they are, they are instead dissected and discussed about as if they are apples. This well-meaning but erroneous trend has translated over into past efforts in creating a written system for sign language.

This textbook proposes a new path, with a special set of terms, towards an accurate representation of ASL on paper.

Fundamentals of ASL Writing

Written ASL begins with the writer, not the reader, nor the observer. Everything that is written down is from the writer's, or signer's, point of view. This sets ASL writing apart from other past efforts towards putting ASL on paper, since they all have been largely based on a descriptive approach of signs.

The written system of ASL outlined in this textbook depends on the internal dialogue of the writer, much like English writing is directed solely by the thoughts and perspective of the writer. The writing system is not intended to be an instruction manual of how to sign ASL, nor is it an exact representative of the author signing to the reader.

Since written English is not a system that outlines how to speak but a vehicle to convey thoughts, written ASL is a way to express thoughts in written form.

Another important aspect of ASL writing is the freedom given to the writer to choose between appropriate digits and marks to convey his/her thoughts in however way he/she prefers.

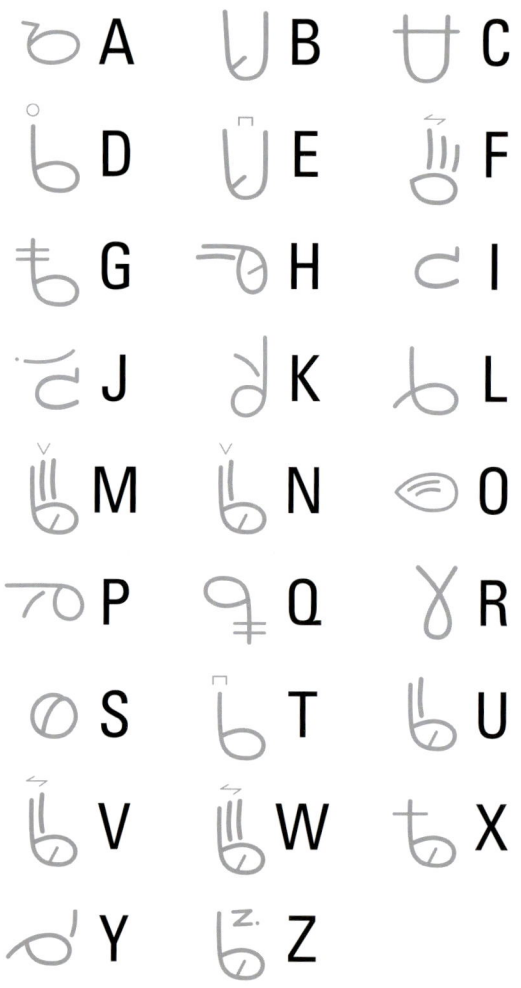

Right-handed digibet next to written English alphabet

The functions of two modal languages

Sign Language: American	Vocal Language: English
Digibet	Alphabet
Digit	Letter
Spacabulary (spatial)	Vocabulary (vocal)
Graph/Word	Word

This flexibility in ASL writing will help young ASL users learn how to compose a text well and to refine how they express their thoughts on paper. They can then apply this process of writing, revising, and editing to written English.

Above all, ASL writing is an internal process, not a notational writing system. Past attempts at writing systems for ASL have been largely notational and heavily dependent on the perspective of the observer of a signer.

Not so with written ASL, which puts the power of the pen directly into the signer's hands. A document in written ASL will reflect a writer's signing style, personality, word choice, and all the nuances of his/her ASL use, all intact from mind to text.

As an end result, the power of the pen lies in your hand. You are the writer.

ASL consists of five main parameters. See the chart below to compare the elements of both modalities of ASL.

Manual ASL	Written ASL
handshape	digit
palm orientation	locative orientation & diacritic
movement	movement line & endpoint
location	locative mark
non-manual signals	non-manual signal mark
	indicator mark*

* The **indicator** mark is a grammatical element that identifies pronouns, time, verbs, and pauses, as well as role shifts and spatial reference.

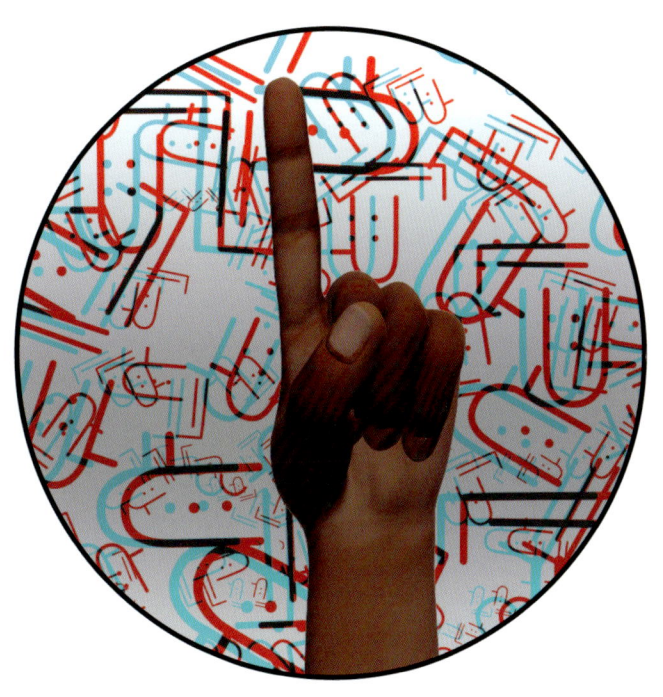

Chapter One

The Digibet

The American Sign Language **digibet** offers a way to write and express thoughts that were originated in ASL and to keep them as intact as possible, without the loss of any meaning or essence inherent in the message.

As discussed in the introduction, the ASL writing system is set in the signer's, and thus the writer's, point of view. This writing system will also allow the writer to use one's dominant hand, since signers sign differently depending on whether they're left-handed or right-handed. Much like cartography in map production, this distinction between the left and right digits gives ASL writing a feeling of three-dimensionality. The reader will know whether the writer is left-handed or right-handed, and from there, further contextual interpretations of the text can be made.

Left and Right

The ASL digibet comes in pairs of left and right digits. Writers will be able to choose from the **digit** pairs as they write, which is a unique feature that no other written language possess.

Orientation, one of the five parameters of ASL, can be difficult to describe in a writing system. However, since orientation can affect meaning, it is an important aspect of ASL that should not be overlooked. The ASL writing system, with its left and right digit pairs, presents a solution that helps both the writer and the reader discern the orientation of signs.

The possibilities for meaningful use of the left and right digits include word play, precise descriptions, stylized writing, and many other writing techniques.

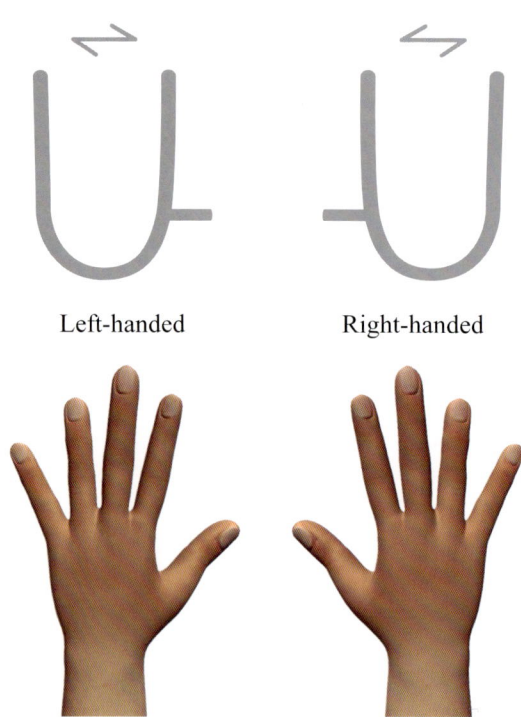

Left-handed   Right-handed

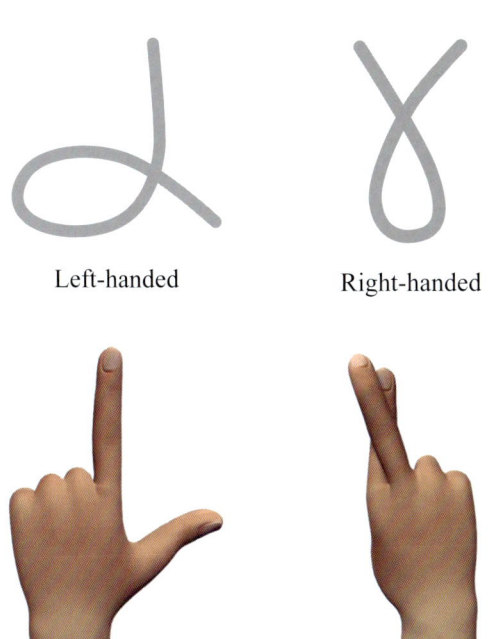

Left-handed   Right-handed

Dominant Digit: Left or Right

As the writer, it's up to you which dominant digit you prefer to use. For example, you may find it easier to use the left digits if you are a left-handed signer. Once you have chosen your dominant digit, that digit will "lead the dance" of the supportive digit as you write the text. This feature will help you to truly think in ASL as you write, just like you're signing right there on paper.

Consistency with your choice of dominant digit throughout the text is vital, which will allow for accurate interpretation when it is read. Also, this will help the reader to be able to truly visualize the writer signing, making reading a text in ASL akin to a 3-D experience.

Thumb Mark

The thumb mark helps establish whether a digit is left or right. Look at the images on the right to see the difference between a left-handed signer and a right-handed signer signing WAIT A MINUTE.

The thumb marks on the two digits shown in the example are in different positions, clearly illustrating whether the signer/writer is left-handed or right-handed.

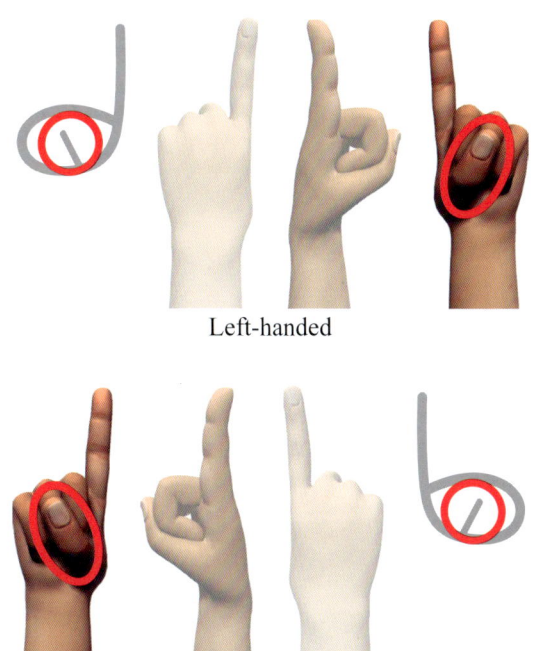

Left-handed

Right-handed

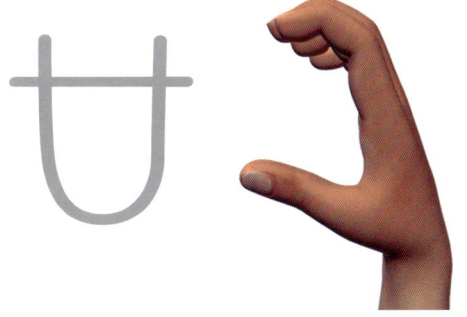

Sans Thumb Mark

A digit without a thumb mark indicates a thumb extending straight outward.

Front Locative Marks

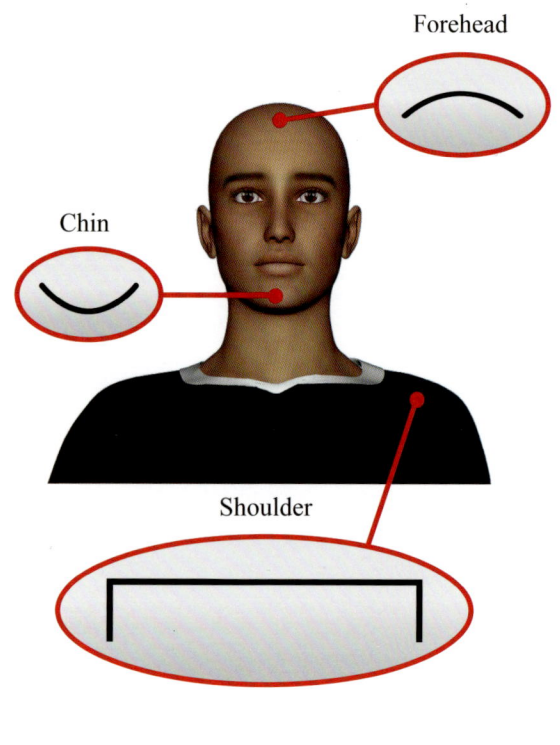
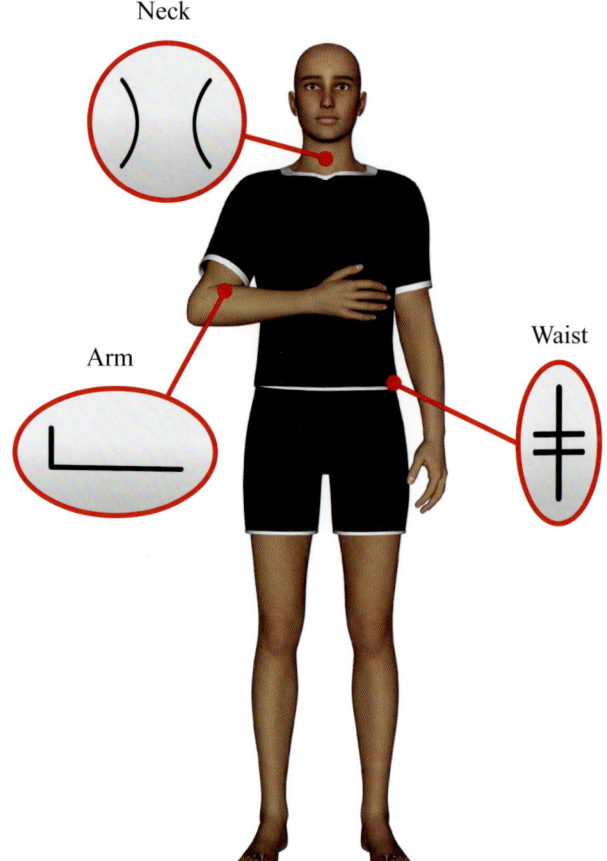

Side Locative Marks

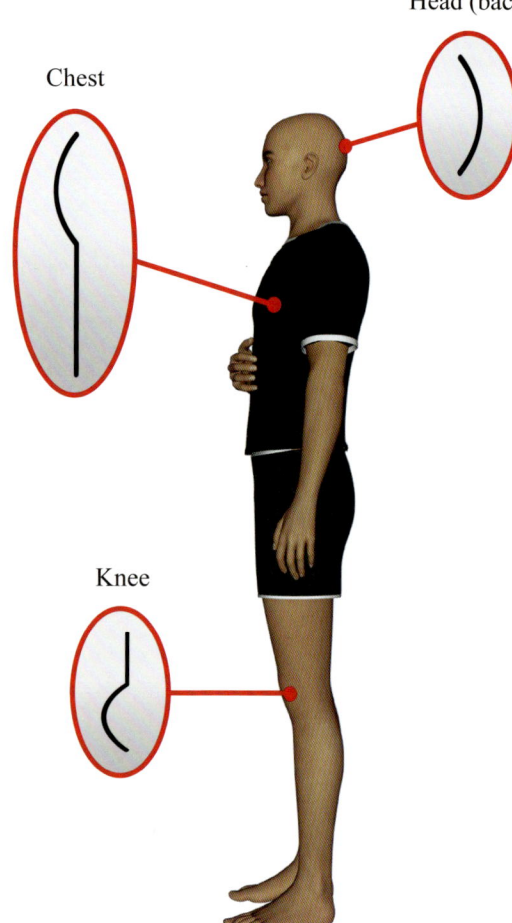
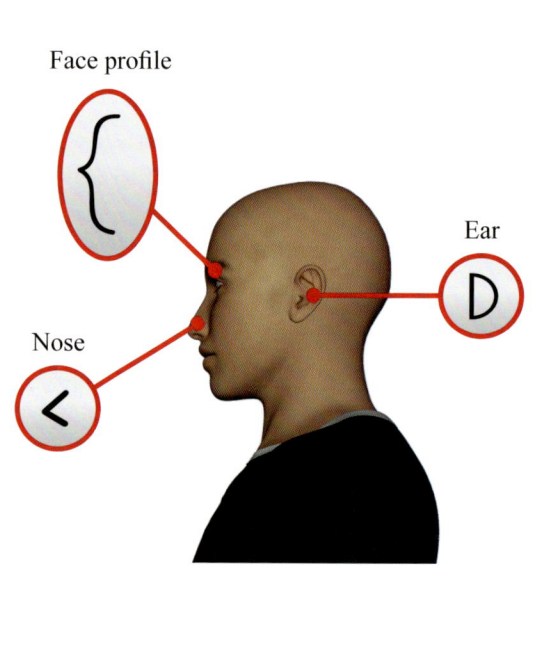

Digits

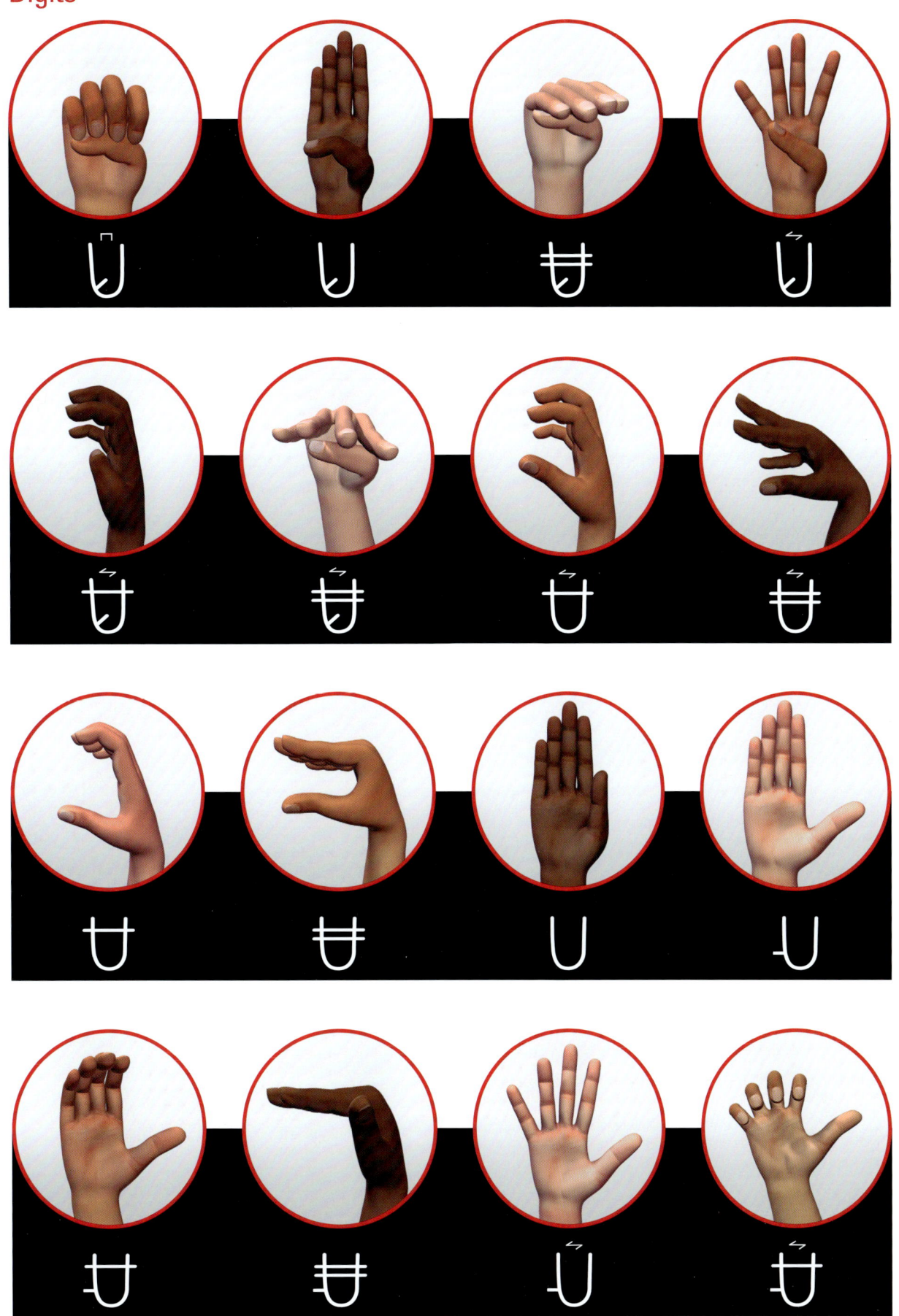

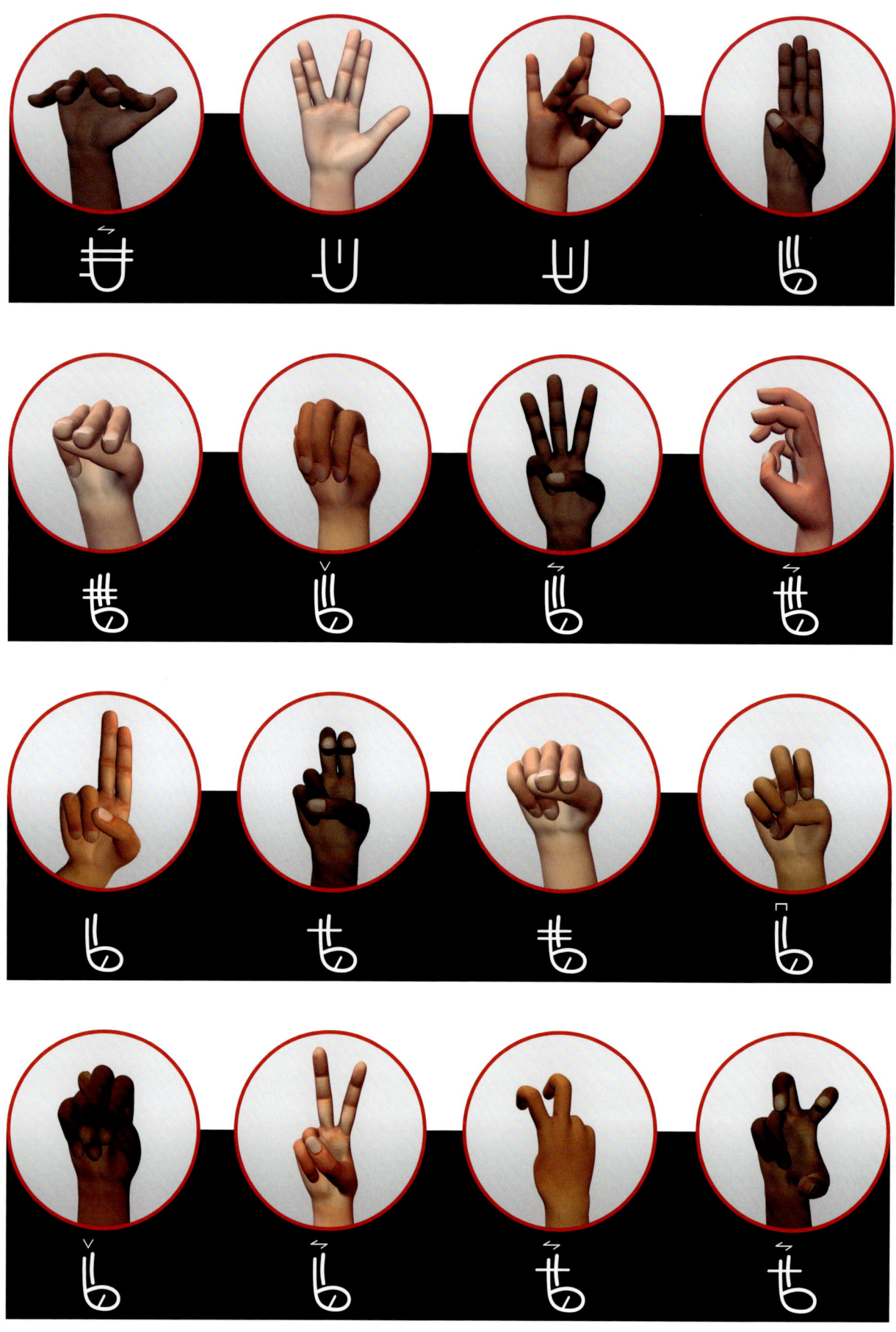

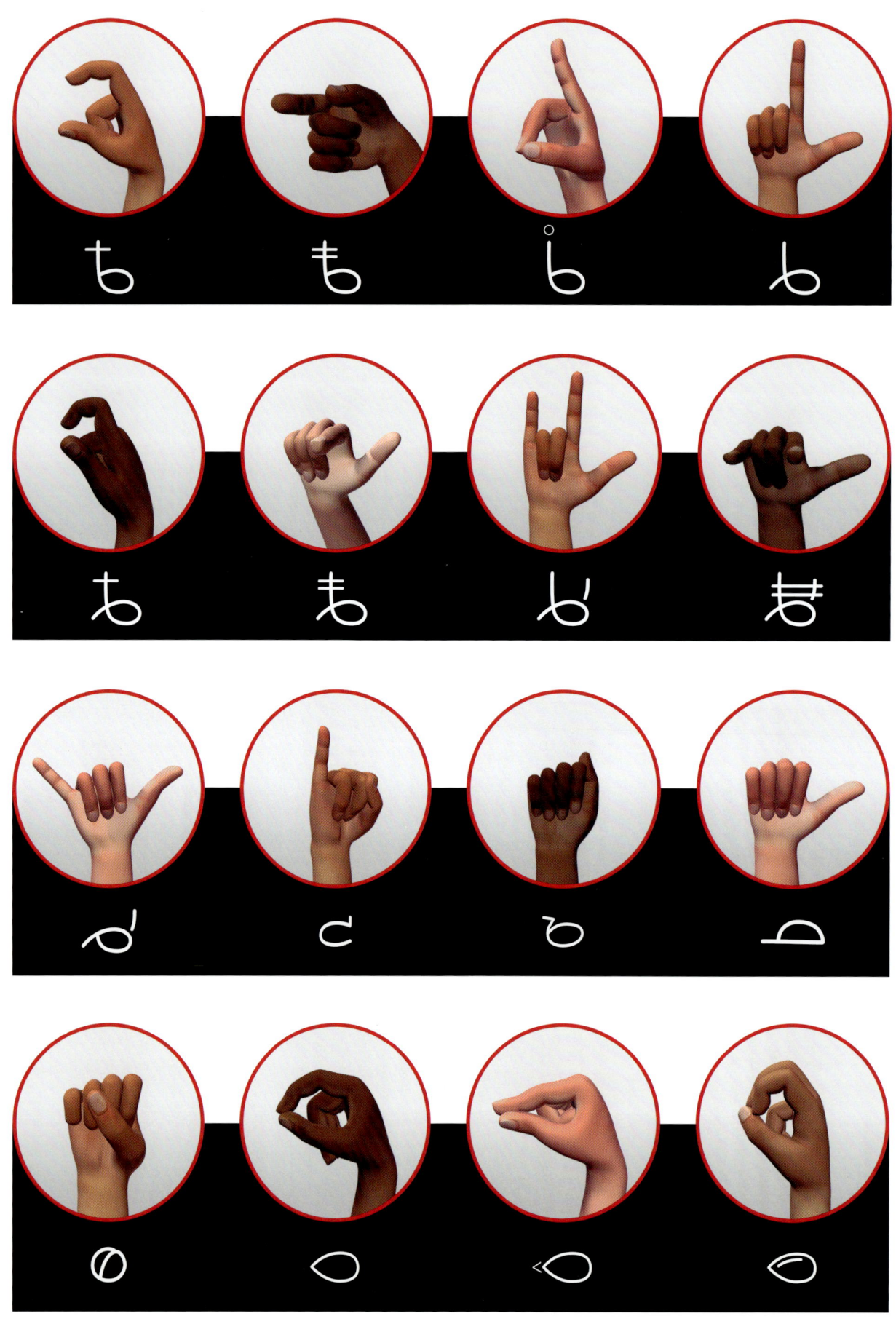

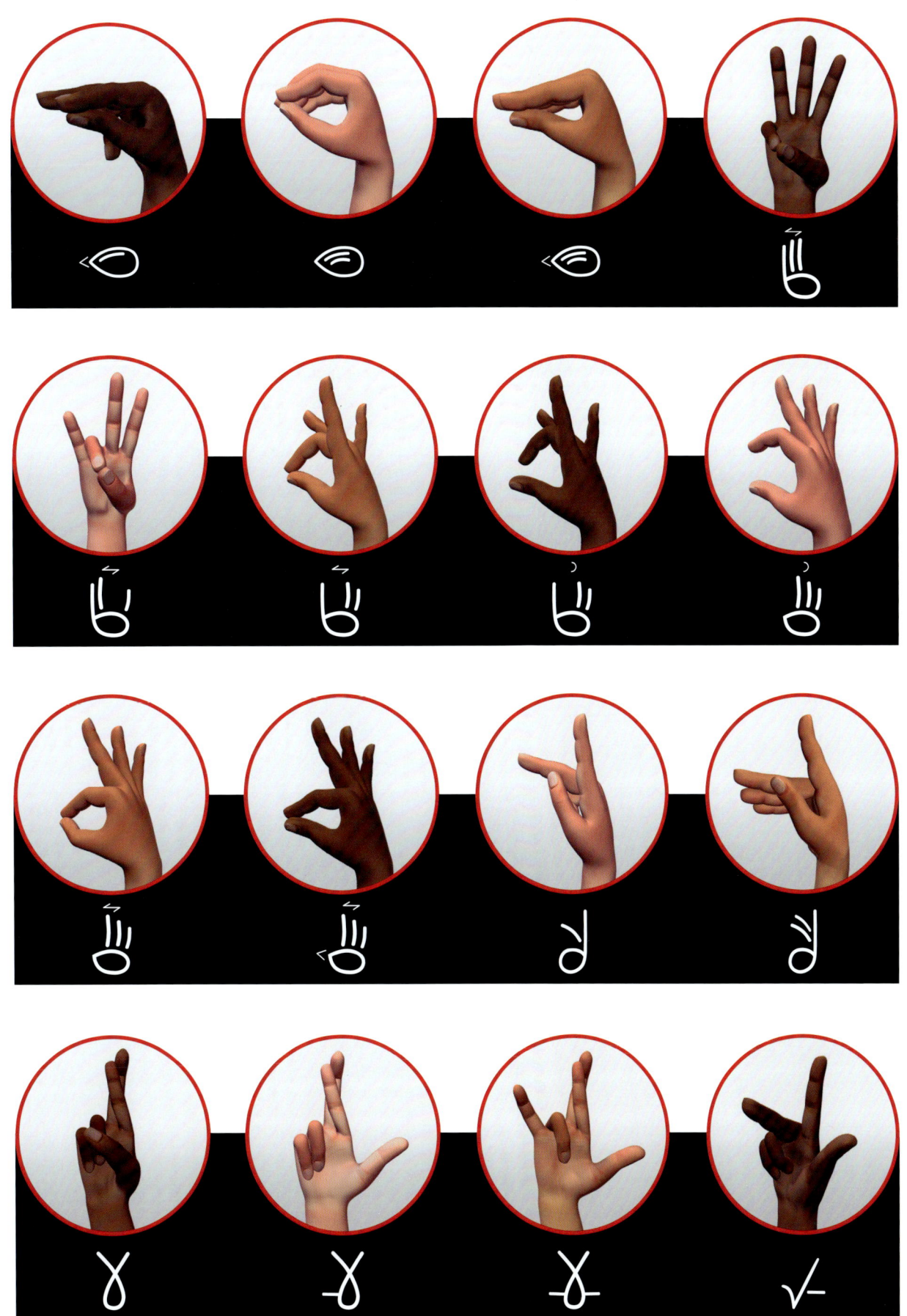

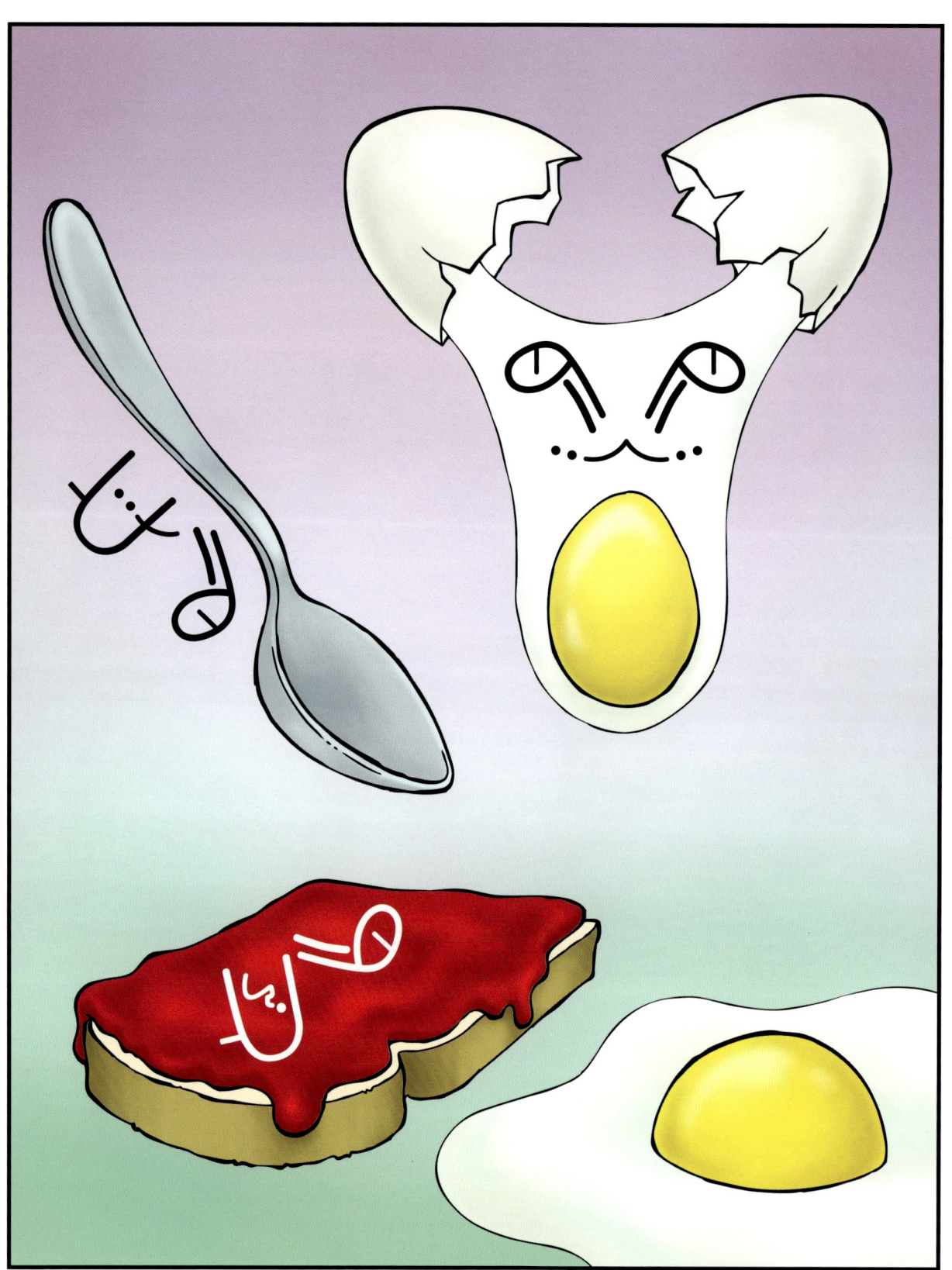

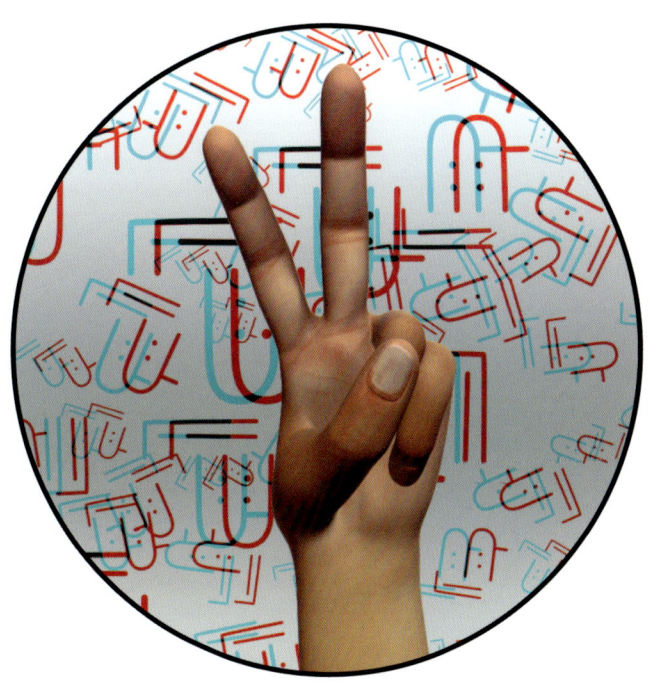

Chapter Two

Diacritic Marks and Endpoints

In most written languages, a diacritic mark above or below a letter or symbol indicates a difference in **pronunciation**. In written ASL, a **diacritic** mark represents the movement of the digit, or the hand.

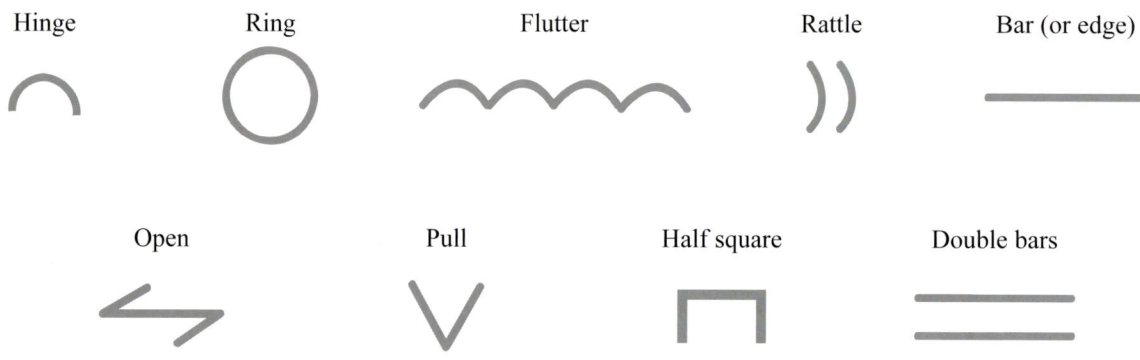

Hinge Diacritic

The **hinge diacritic** is written as a half-arc symbol, which represents two functions:

1. a sideways or back-and-forth digit motion. The specific motion depends on the context of the word in a sentence. The signs WHERE, which has a sideways motion, and MUST, which has a back-and-forth motion, both use the hinge diacritic. This diacritic is placed at the bottom of a digit, and

2. a halfway closure where one or two fingers almost touch the thumb tip. Signs that use this shape include EARTH (dominant hand). This diacritic is placed at the top, or finger tip region, of the digit.

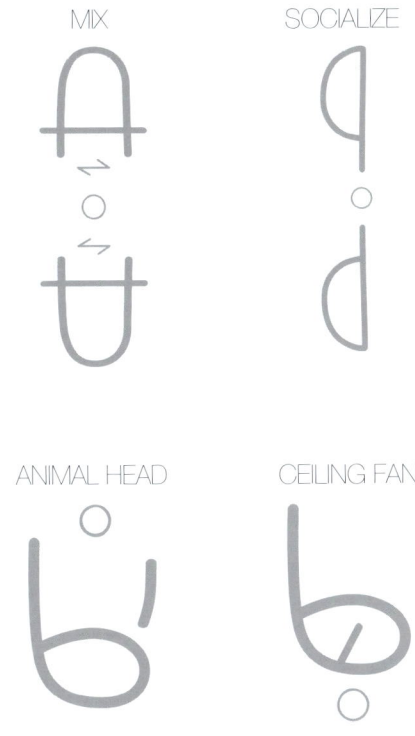

Ring Diacritic

The **ring diacritic** is a circular symbol that represents three basic functions:

1. a rotating wrist-digit motion. Signs that use this movement include CEILING FAN and WHEEL. The ring diacritic is placed below, or in the wrist region, of a digit,

2. a closure of two or three fingers touching the thumb tip. Signs that use this shape include an animal head with two ears or the handshape D. This is placed at the top, or finger tip region, of the digit, and

3. a rotation of two digits simultaneously. This is seen in the signs SOCIALIZE and MIX.

Flutter Diacritic

The **flutter diacritic** indicates the wiggling of two or more fingers simultaneously, but not together. This diacritic is placed at the top of the digit, where the fingers are. It is not necessary to write the open diacritic with the flutter diacritic as it serves the same function to indicate split fingers.

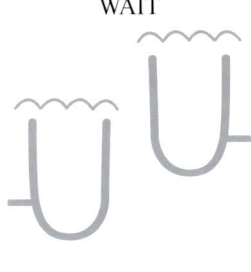

WAIT

EITHER

COLOR

FINGERSPELLING

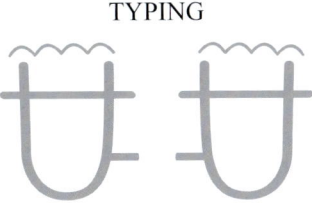

TYPING

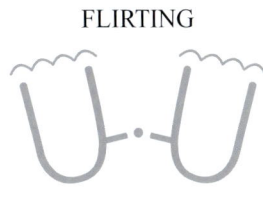

FLIRTING

Pull Diacritic

The **pull diacritic** is used to represent a pull direction of fingers away from the palm. The signs are MONEY, HAIR PIN, CAT and handshape N. This diacritic is placed at the finger and thumb tip region of the digit.

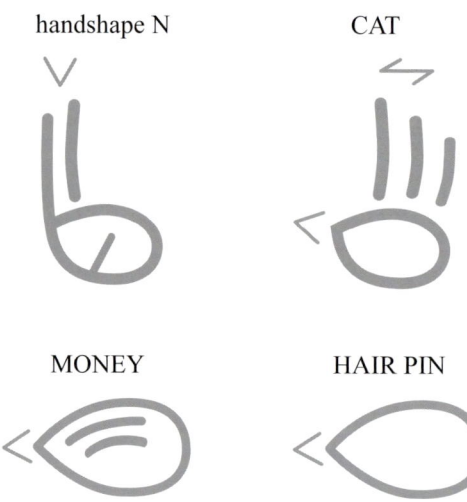

Half Square Diacritic

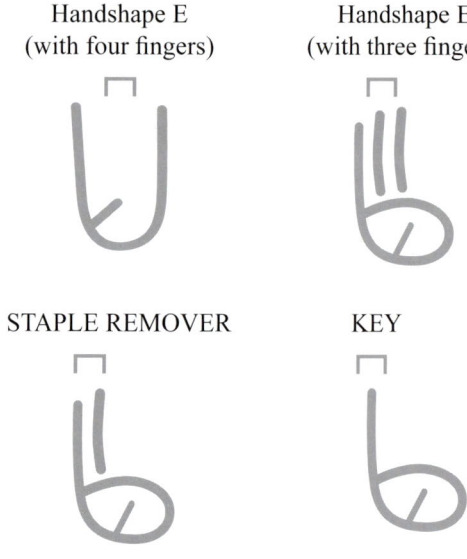

The **half-square diacritic** indicates one or more fingers folded to rest on a closed thumb. The signs are E (with four fingers), E (with three fingers), E (with 2 fingers), and bent handshape This diacritic is placed at the top, or finger tip region, of the digit.

Rattle Diacritic

The **rattle diacritic** indicates the shaking of one or more fingers, or the whole hand. The rattle diacritic is placed anywhere around the digit depending on where the motion is most visible.

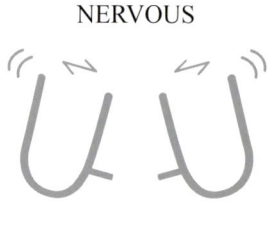

Open Diacritic

The **open diacritic**, as placed at the top of the digit, indicates fingers split. The signs are handshape V, CLAW, handshape F and CLIMB.

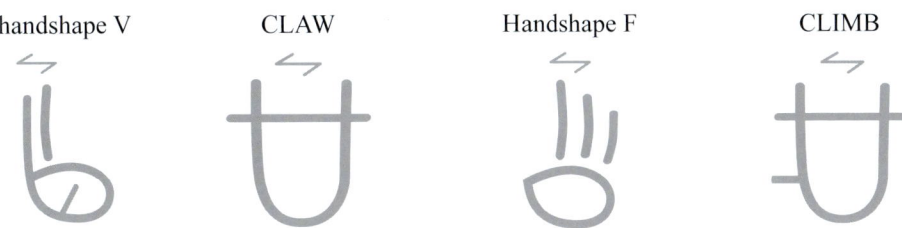

Bar (or Edge) Diacritic

The **bar diacritic** represents two functions:

1. indicates one or more bent fingers at the upper finger joint. The signs are SHOULD, POTATO (dominant hand), BALL and STARE. This diacritic is placed across the upper part of the digit.

2. shows the orientation of the hand, or digit, in a sign. See HALLWAY and PLANNING.

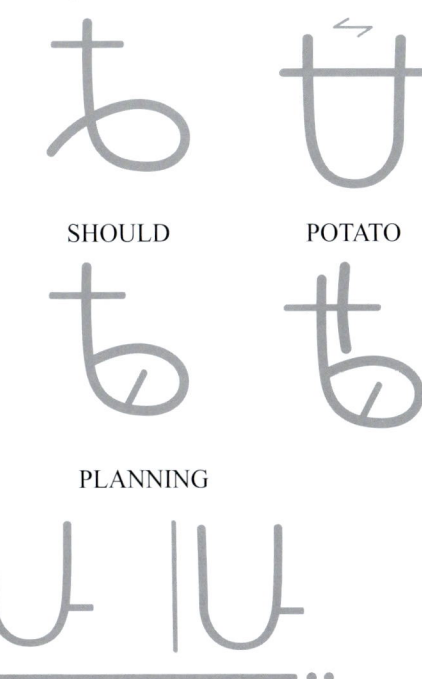

Double Bars Diacritic

The **double bars diacritic**, as placed across the upper part of the digit, indicates one or more bent fingers at the lower finger joint. The signs are EXPECT, FUNNY, AIRPORT and MOSQUITO.

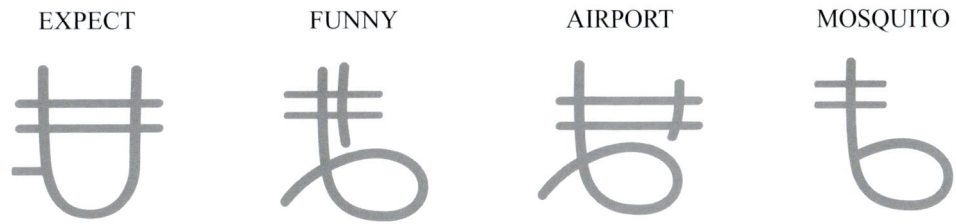

Endpoints

Single movements are called uninflected motions and they tend to indicate a verb. Double movements, or repetitive motions, are often used for nouns. Three or more movements, or continuous motions, are usually used with action verbs. Directional, or inflective, motions are seen in directional verbs, nouns, or action words.

Verb, Noun and Action Endpoints

The number of endpoints indicates whether a sign is a verb, noun, or reptitive action. The dot represents as the **endpoint**.

One motion

| STOP | ON TIME | FAST |

Two motions

| SCHOOL | DEAF SCHOOL | EVERYDAY |

Three or more motions

Diacritic Marks with Endpoints

Diacritic marks are used in written ASL to indicate wrist and digit motion. Endpoints can be added to diacritic marks to represent repeated motions.

You can add as many endpoints as you would like to a diacritic to make a certain emphasis. For instance, if you're describing the act of trying to start a car on a cold morning by turning the car key several times, you could add another endpoint to convey a sense of frustration.

Chapter Three

Movement Line and Morphs

Movements are widely used in ASL and a change in motion can mean a difference in definition, **inflection**, **grammar**, and more. There are three basic directions that can be used by the signer/writer: horizontal, vertical, and distance. More complicated directions are written with the help of **locative marks**.

Movement Line and Endpoint

The **movement line** and endpoint indicates the direction of signs. The line acts as a track and the endpoint shows where the motion is going.

To indicate left and right movements, write a horizontal line with a dot at either the left or right and place it below the digit(s). Think of the arrows that you see on highway signs. The dot at the end of the line acts in the same way as the point on an arrow does.

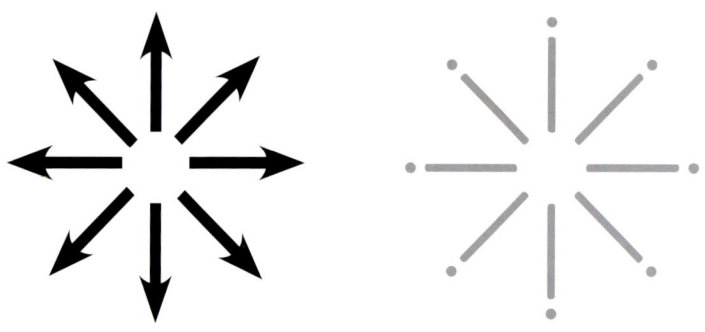

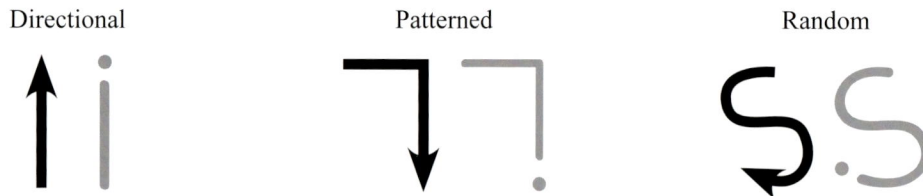

Directional   Patterned   Random

For up-down and left-right movements, use any front locative mark and and line with a dot at the end.

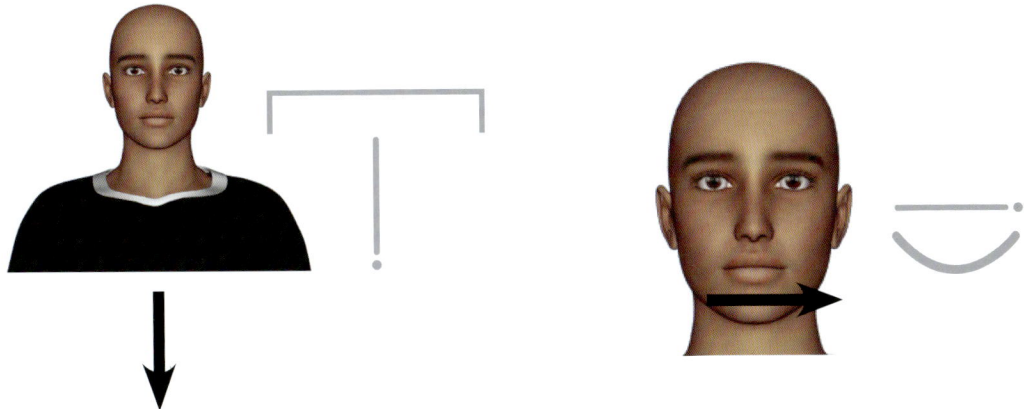

For forward-backward movements, use any side locative mark and line with a dot at the end.

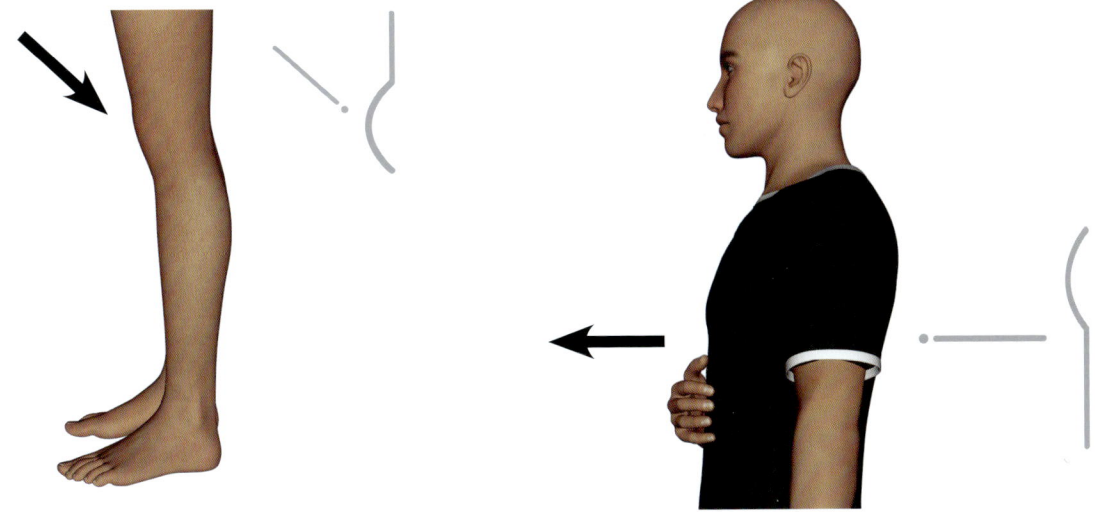

Directional Movement

Use a vertical movement line when writing upward and downward movements with an endpoint and a horizontal line for left and right.

NORTH   SOUTH   EAST   WEST

Patterned Movement

This movement line indicates that the digit moves in a predictable direction. This is commonly found in nouns, especially those that refer to a place, such as city names.

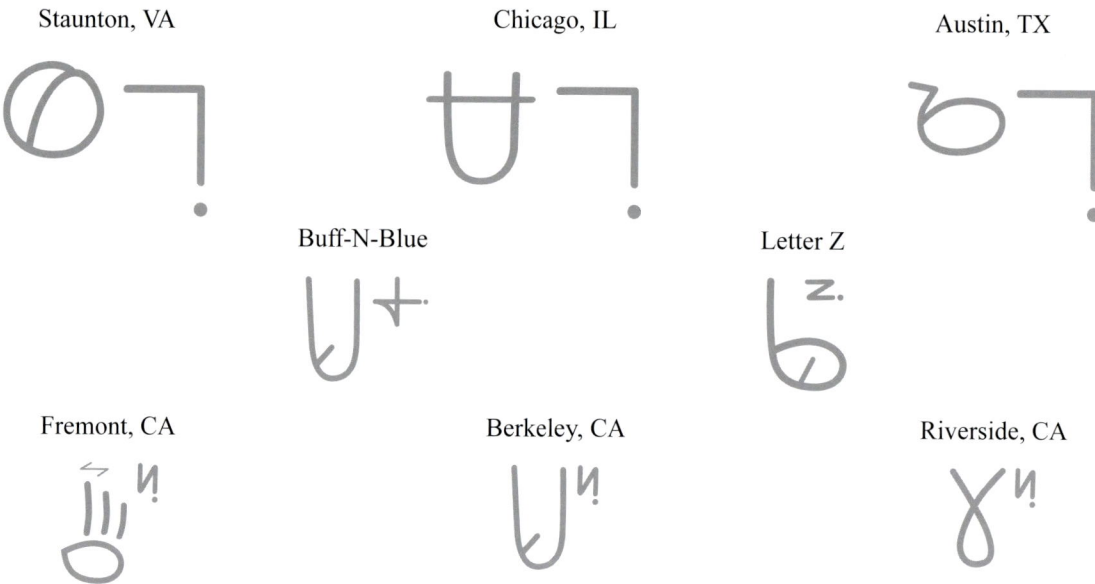

Random Movement

This movement is unrestricted and can be expressed in any form determined by the writer. Random movement lines would be used for leaf falling and rolling in the wind, airline flight having a bumpy ride, and balloon drifting higher in the wind, to name a few examples.

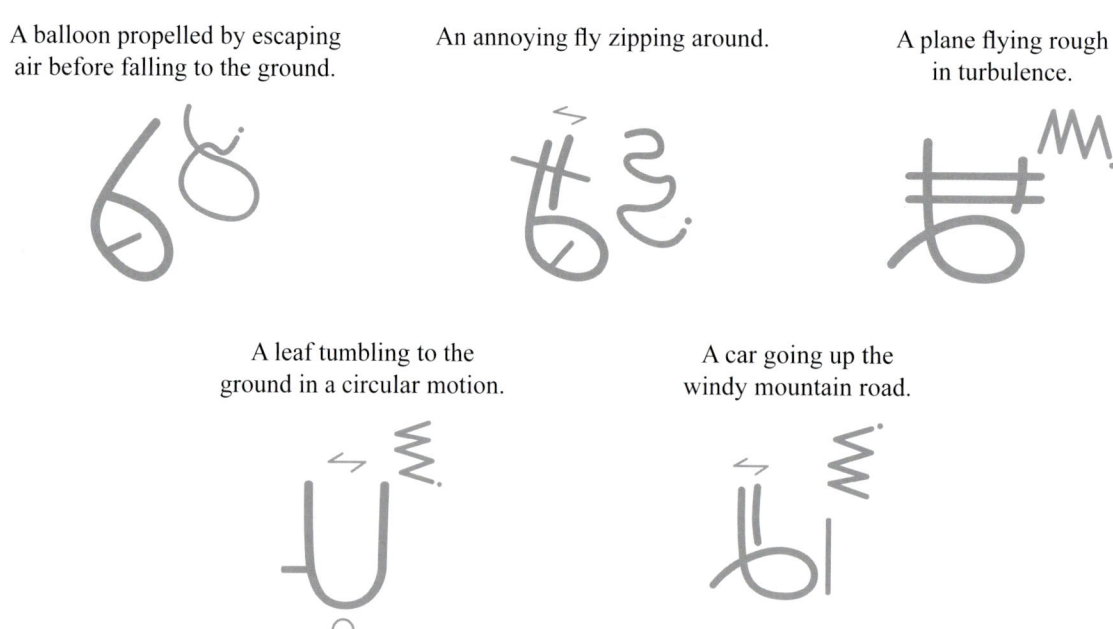

Other motions

There are signs indicating the motion of two digits like MEET and WITH. The dot between two lines indicates a meeting point of two digits.

A dash on the line indicates the split of the two digits, moving away from each other. You use this when writing SEPARATE and OPPOSITE.

Alternating Mark

The **alternating mark**, which resembles a half arrow tip, shows which handshape moves first in a sign. There must be at least two endpoints above the mark to represent repetition.

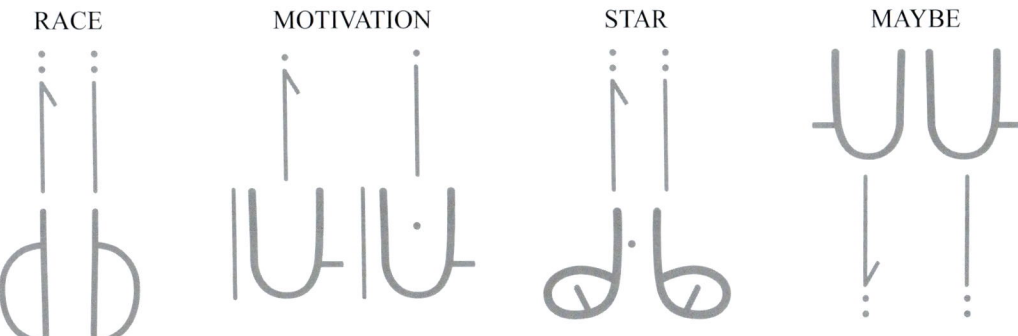

Repeating Movement Lines and Endpoints

Out to three or more people

To three or more of us

Three or more people to self

Three or more of us to a person

A woman handing out surveys to people

Palm Orientation and Movement Line Combination

Palm orientation, which refers to the positioning of the hands, is one of the most flexible aspects of ASL. This flexibility is reflected in the written system of ASL, where the digit can be moved around and modified in countless ways with the help of the movement line.

However, most signs follow certain patterns that adhere to the language structure of sign language. These patterns are translated into codes that can be easily written.

Exchanging bowls

Two persons walking by each other

Two birds flying by each other

A car moving forward

A car moving backward

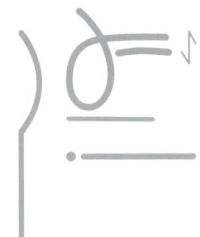

A car coming to you

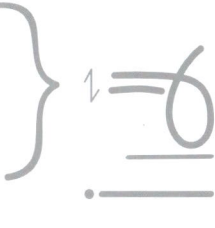

A car plunging over a cliff

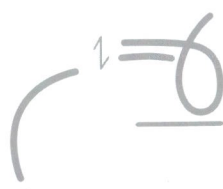

A car flipping over in the air

Motion Morphs

A **morphing** digit is when a digit morphs from one shape to another in one continuous flow. Sometimes a morphing digit can morph into three, four, or even five different handshapes. The morphing action can happen while in motion or in stationary form.

EARLY

EARLY

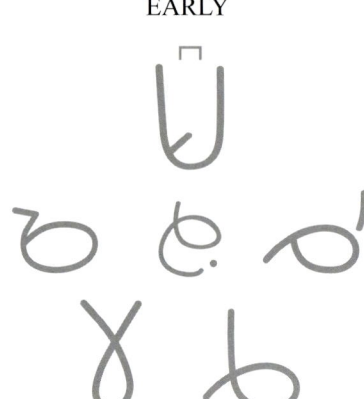

A person thinking of food

NUMEROUS

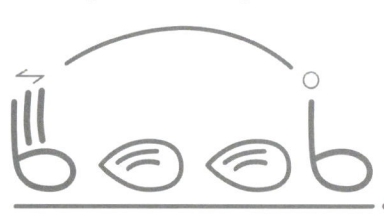
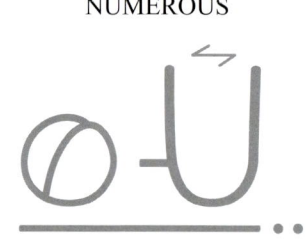

UNDERSTAND

DISAPPEAR

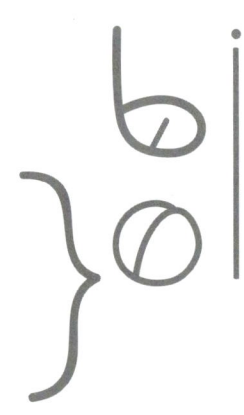
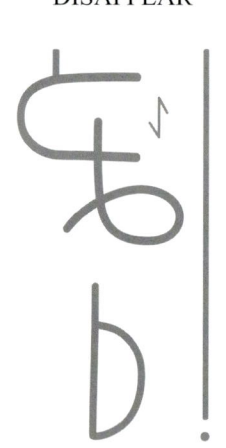

Stationary Morphs

Stationary morphs do not move in space. They are anchored in one spot. A stationary morph is written with a dot underneath the movement line. This dot is called an anchor point. Think of it as a nail that holds the morph in place.

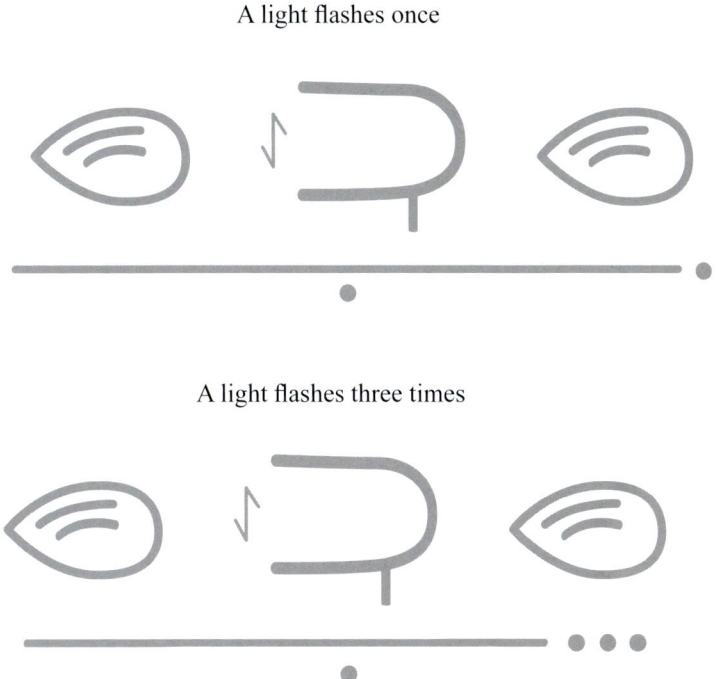

Some digits can be neatly combined by overlapping the left and right versions, as seen below, while some others will need to be joined together in unique ways, like in the signs ABBREVIATION/SUMMARIZE, YELL/SCOLD and FRIENDS.

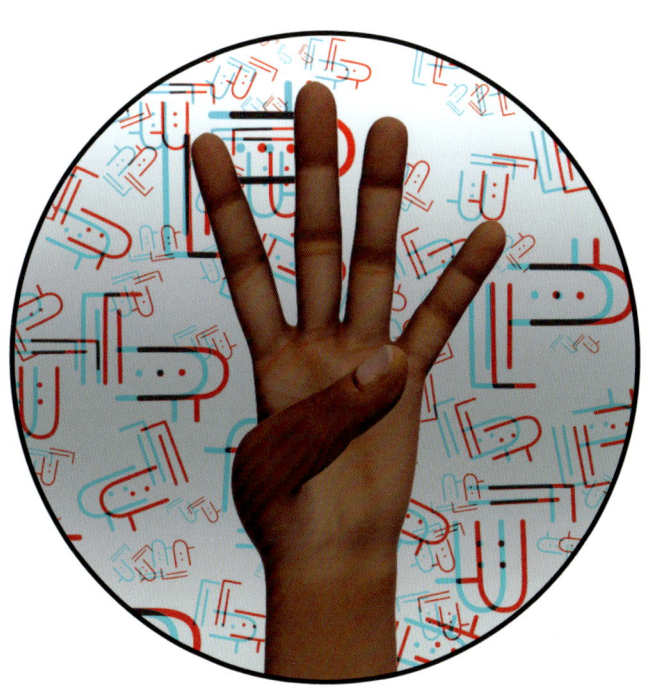

Chapter Four

Non-Manual Signals

Non-manual signals, or NMS marks, are facial expressions that add information to words and sentences in ASL. They can determine the structure of a sentence, add inflection to signs, change the meaning of a message, and act as other linguistic functions. NMS can also indicate whether a sentence is a question or a statement.

The facial NMS marks in ASL writing are divided into three categories depending on their location on the face: MOUTH, EYEBROW, and NOSE.

Mouth Marks

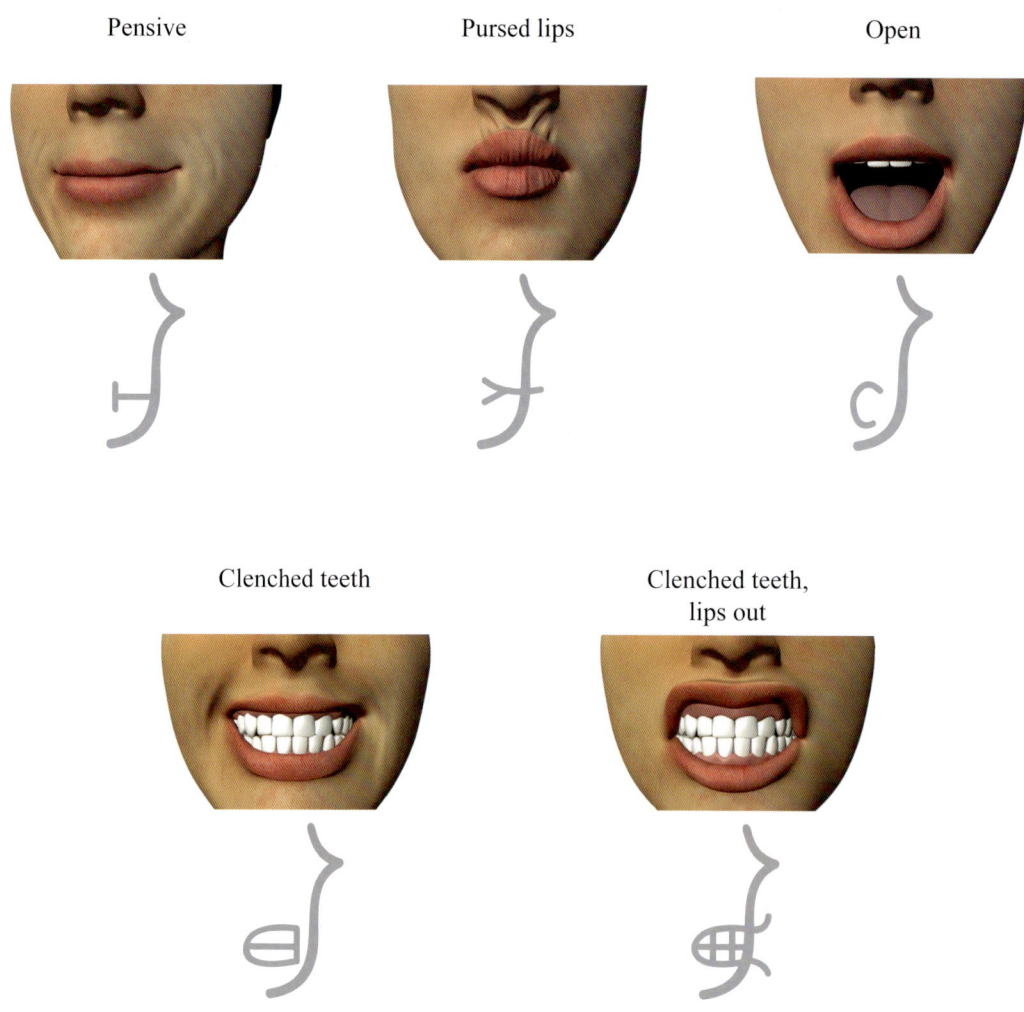

Pensive

Pursed lips

Open

Clenched teeth

Clenched teeth, lips out

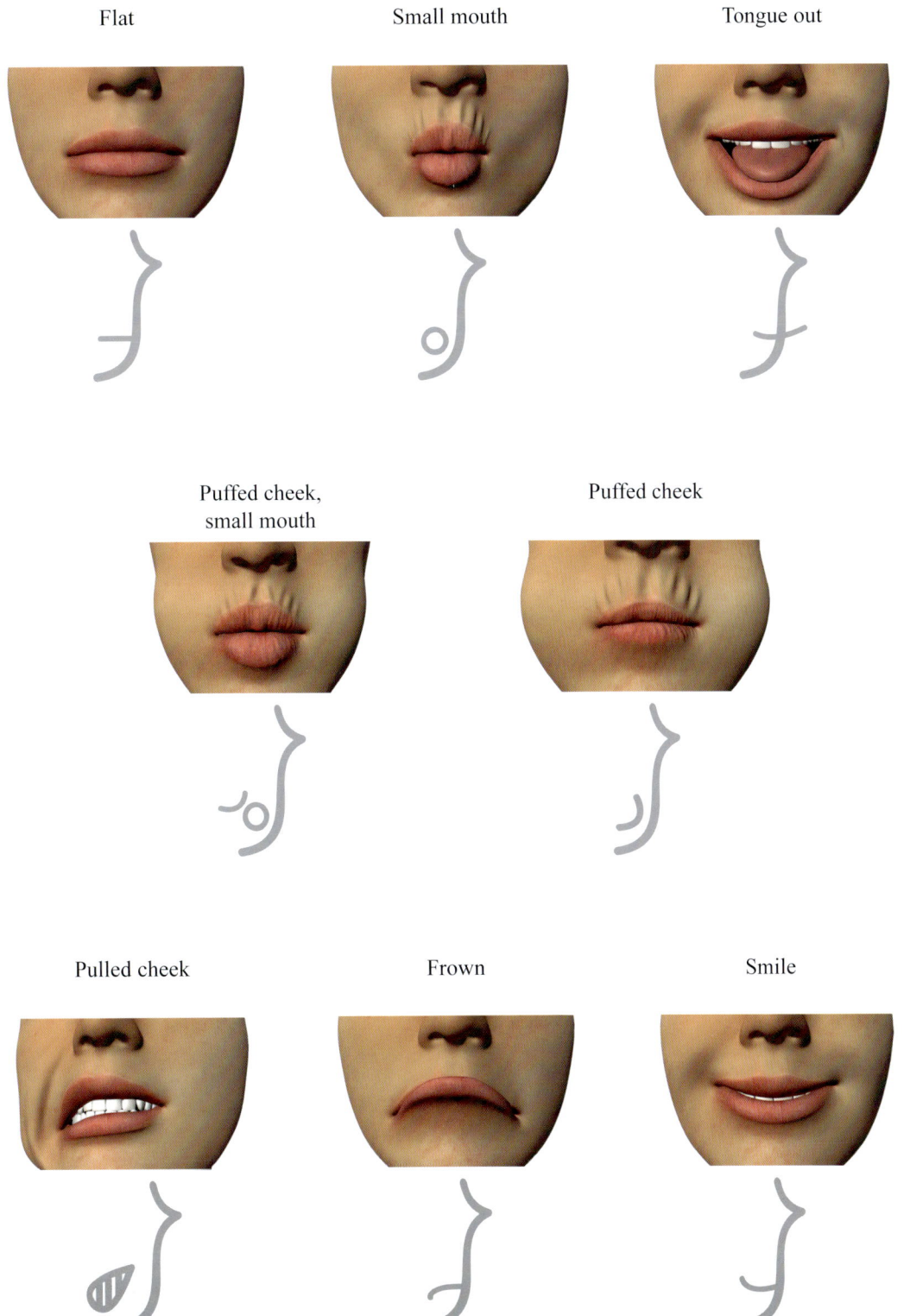

Eyebrow Marks

The WH-question, the lowered eyebrows, is indicated by a "frown" expression.

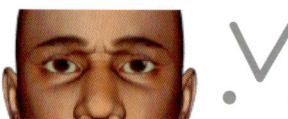

The yes-no, topical, and rhetorical question, the raised eyebrows, is indicated by a "surprise" expression.

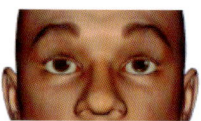 

The WH-question, the lowered eyebrows, is indicated by a "frown" expression.

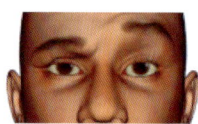 

Nose Marks

The nose crinkle is common in ASL usage to indicate an affirmative (yes) answer or dislike. The nose marker on the left is plain and the one on the right has crinkle lines across it.

WH-Questions

Questions are frequently raised in daily conversations and in writing, making it necessary to establish special symbols for the eight common question words. Shown below are WH-question NMS mark combined with diacritics to indicate a certain question word.

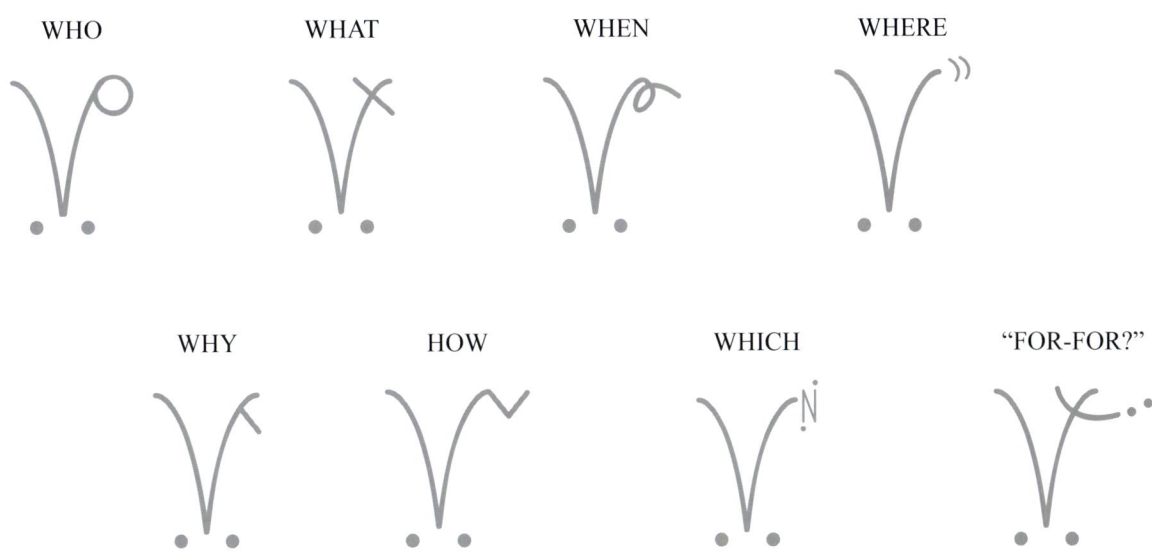

Compound Marks

Eyebrow, nose, and mouth NMS marks can be combined to create a compound NMS mark that accurately reflects the usage in a signed sentence.

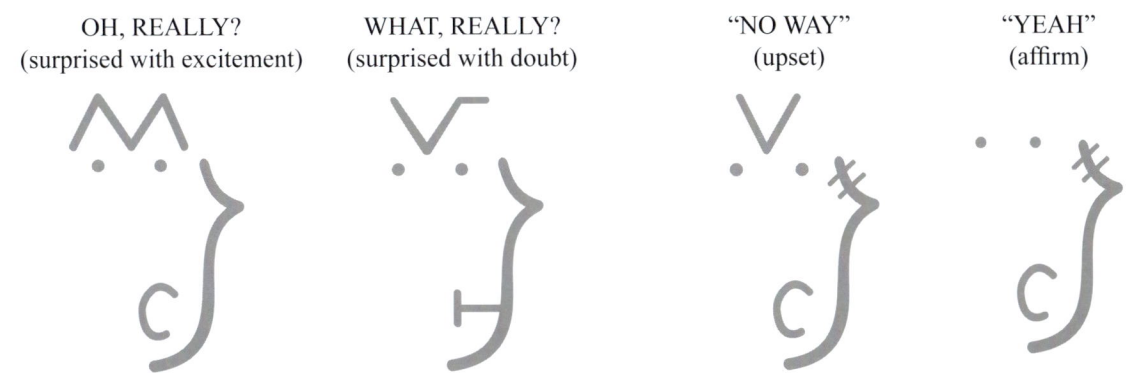

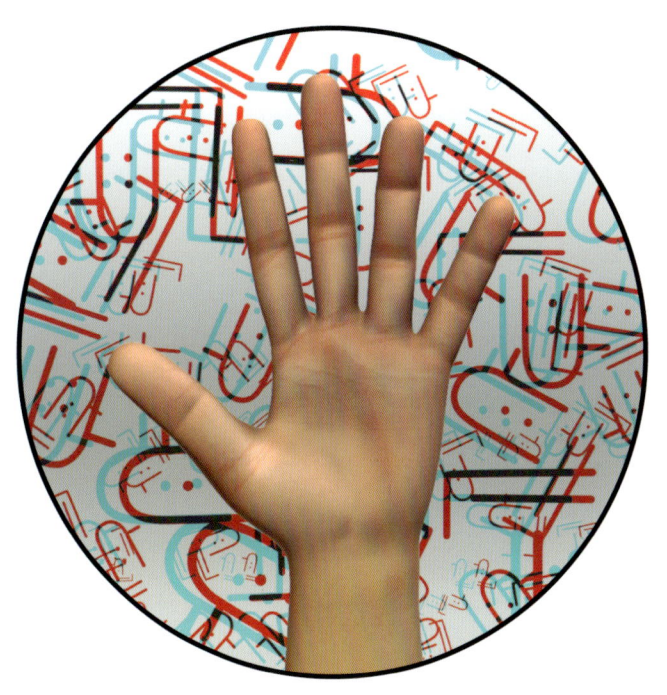

ᜋᜅᜎᜓᜊ᜔ᜃᜓᜌ᜔ ᜎᜒᜎᜒᜋ᜔
Chapter Five

Reserved Marks

Daily conversations in ASL include a lot of pronouns, time indicators, pauses, and other certain words that are used frequently. Since these elements are so often used in ASL, there is a need to establish designated symbols for them to increase the ease of writing. These symbols are called reserved marks. As written ASL gains prominence and becomes more widespread, new reserved marks might be added to the ASL lexicon in the future.

Pronoun Marks

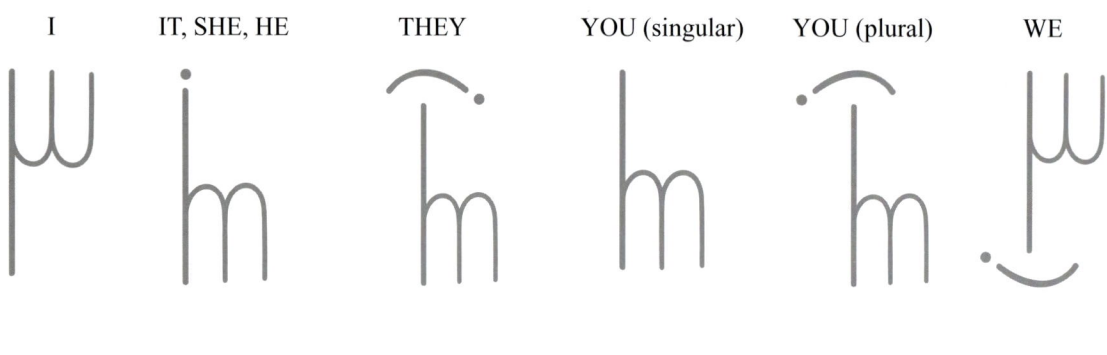

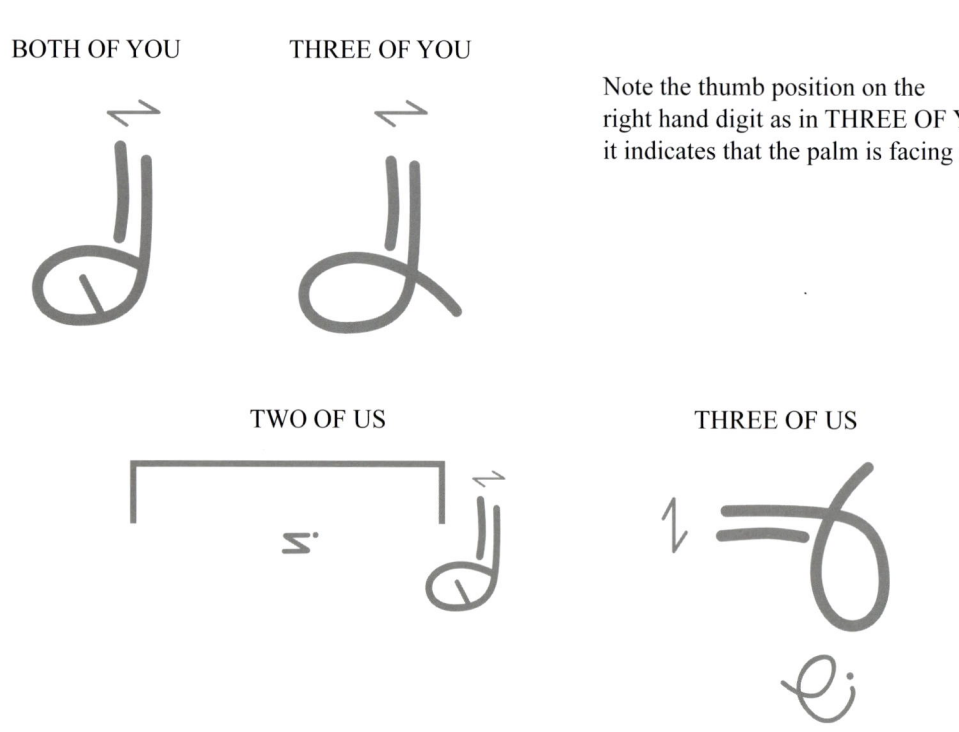

Note the thumb position on the right hand digit as in THREE OF YOU, it indicates that the palm is facing up.

Possessive Pronoun Marks

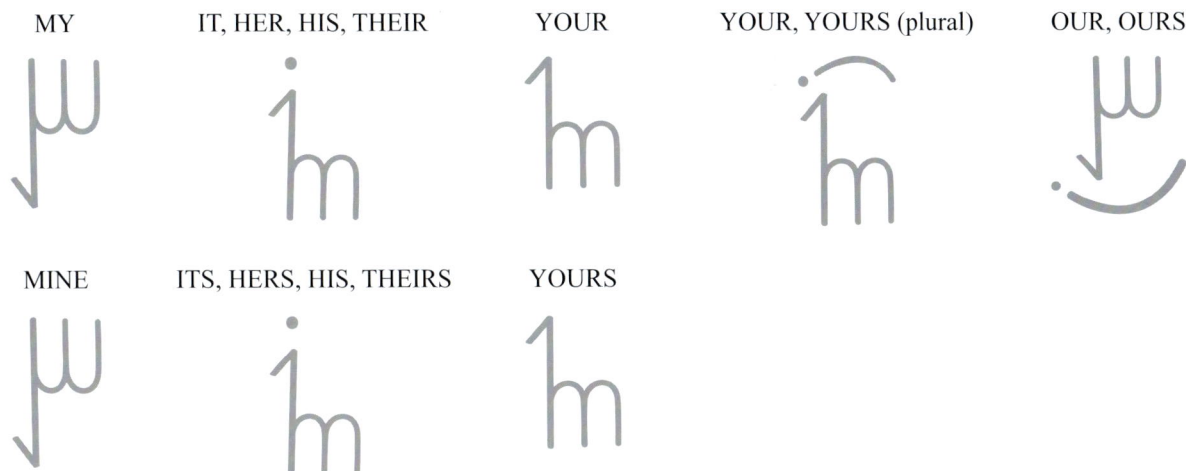

Verb Marks

The verb mark has a simple meaning: go to or come from. This reserved mark is used to represent the concepts of going somewhere, going to a place, coming from somewhere, or coming from a place.

To indicate past, present, or future tense, write a combination of a time indicator mark and the verb mark.

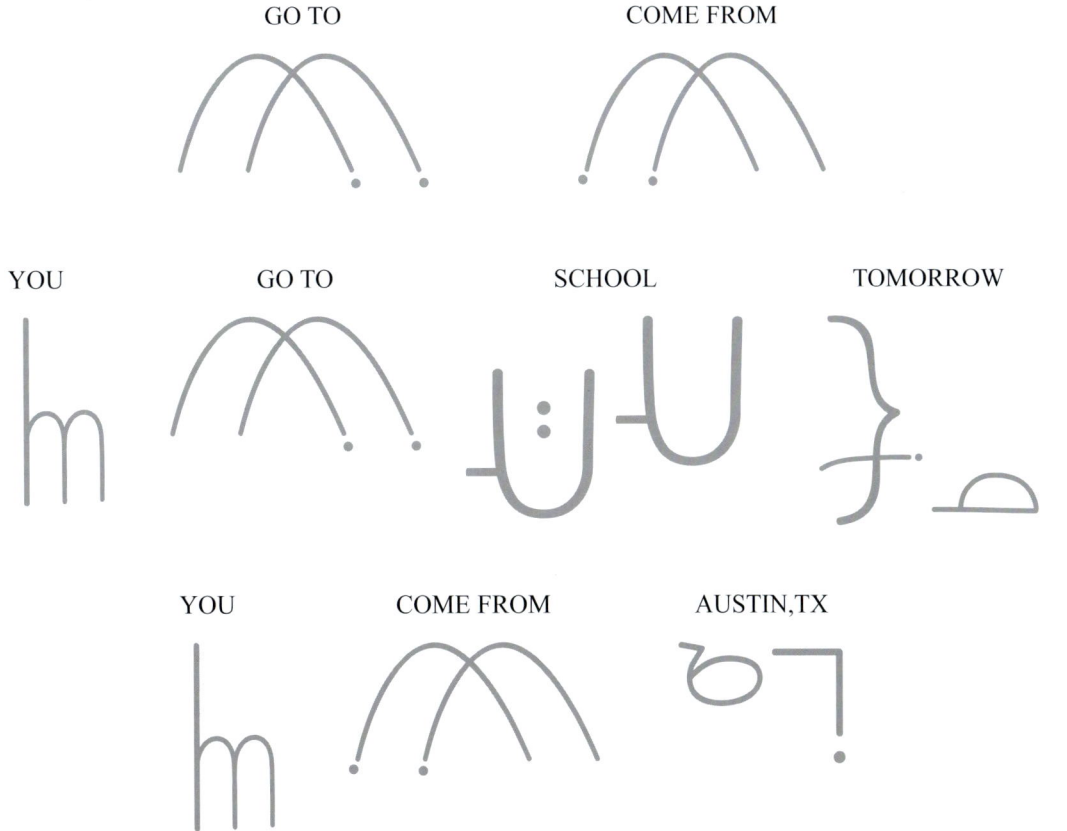

Pause Marks

The pause mark is used to indicate the end of a sentence, a short pause, or a long pause. It is used in a similar way to how the period is used in written English.

PAUSE (end of sentence)

DELAYED PAUSE #1

DELAYED PAUSE #2

Person/People Marks

This reserved mark represents the sign PERSON. Dashes next to the symbol indicate plurality. The person mark can also mean PEOPLE when two dashes are added. Combine the person mark with other signs to indicate a person's role such as DEAF PEOPLE, POET or WRITER.

ONE PERSON	TWO PERSONS	PEOPLE

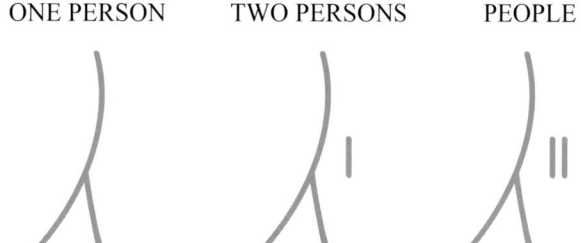

WRITER	TWO POETS	DEAF PEOPLE

 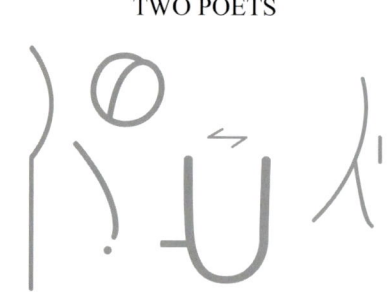 

Time Indicator Marks

References in time is often used in ASL to indicate past, present, and future tense. These time indicators are usually stated at the beginning of ASL sentences.

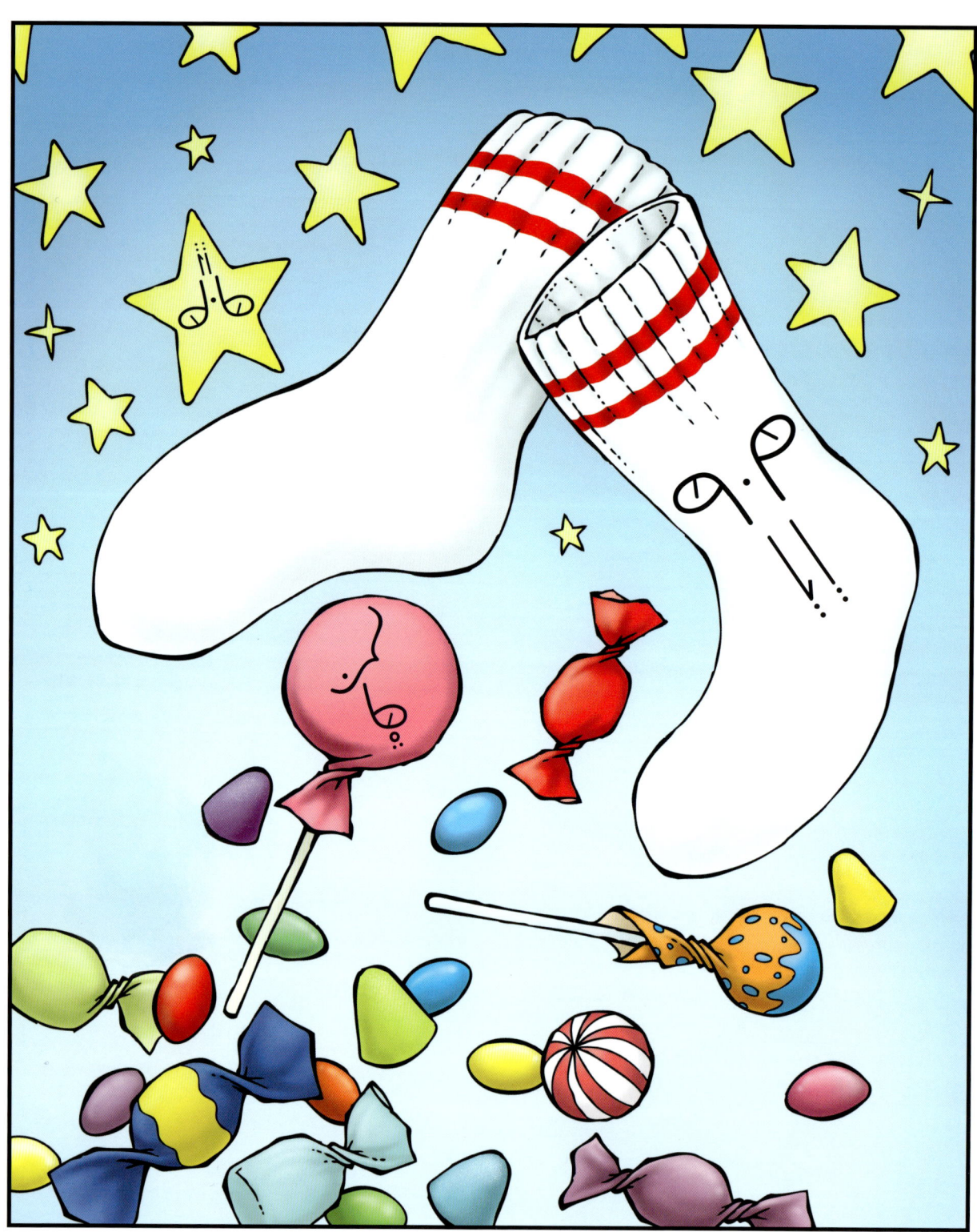

ᙡᖃᖅᑐᒻᒥᖕᒃ ᐅᓄᑉ
Chapter Six

Composition

Now that you know how to use all the parts of ASL writing, you're ready to dive into the actual construction of words and sentences. This chapter will show you how to use non-manual signal marks, locative marks, movement marks, diacritics, and indicator marks to construct a complete sentence in written ASL.

We'll learn the following structures in writing a word and a sentence:

- Placement of digits.
- Placement of the locative marks.
- Placement of non-manual signal marks.
- Placement of the motion line and endpoint.
- Placement of pause marks.

Digits

Locative mark + digit(s) + movement line mark + endpoint

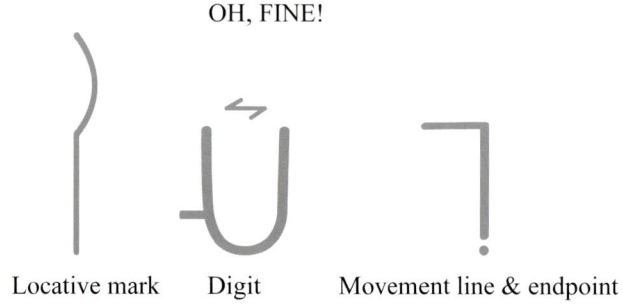

Locative Marks

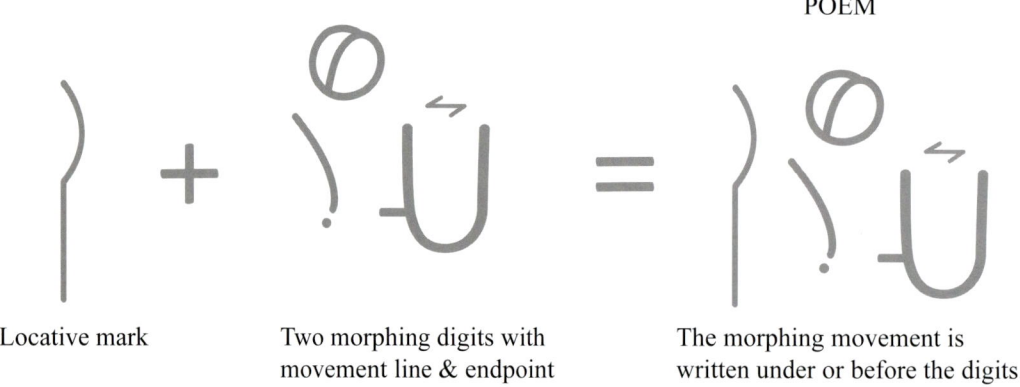

Non-Manual Signal Marks

Non-manual signal (NMS) marks are written in the upper region of the sentence, in a smaller size that is similar to the size of a quotation mark in written English. NMS marks adds vital information to an ASL sentence. They can act as grammatical elements, determine the structure of a sentence, and adjust the tone of a message. NMS marks play a crucial role in the contextual interpretation of a text in written ASL.

The raised eyebrows mark is usually placed at the beginning of a sentence, but they can be written anywhere in a sentence. Since this NMS mark indicates a subject, its placement is a way to inform the reader what the subject of the sentence is.

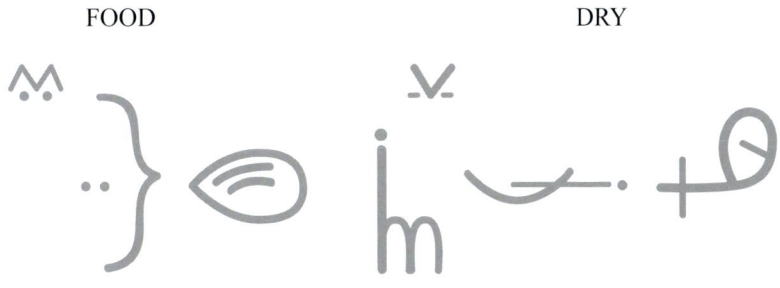

Note that the raised eyebrows mark is placed at the beginning and the frown eyebrows mark is written before CHIN.

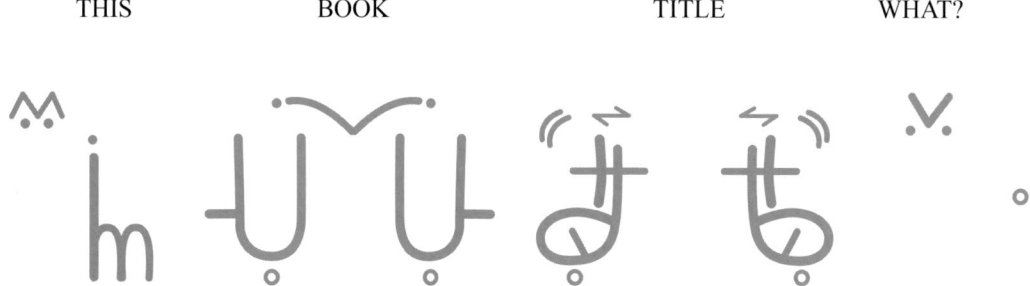

The marks are used to show that a sentence includes one of the seven WH question words: who, what, when, where, why, how, and which. The reader will deduct from the context of the sentence which one of the 7 WH question words is being used in the sentence.

Note the WH NMS mark before ALI. This indicates that the sentence is one of the 7 WH questions.

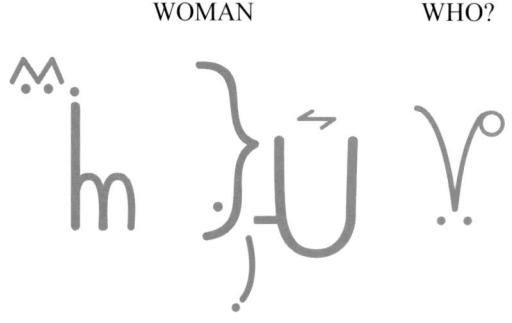

The WHO NMS mark is placed at the end of the sentence. This informs the reader that this sentence is a WH question.

Motion Line and Endpoint

Pause Marks

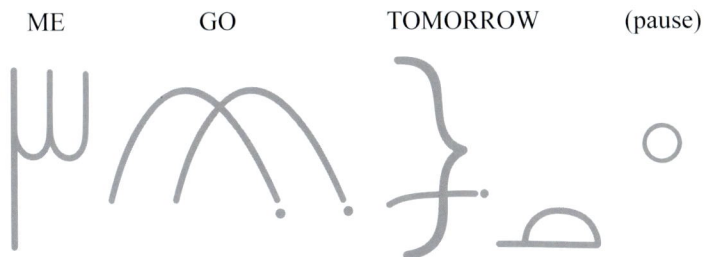

Three pause marks indicate a long pause.

Chapter Seven

Further Readings

George Veditz: The Preservation of American Sign Language

Joseph Davis: Deaf-Blind Ninja

Ella Mae Lentz: The Treasure

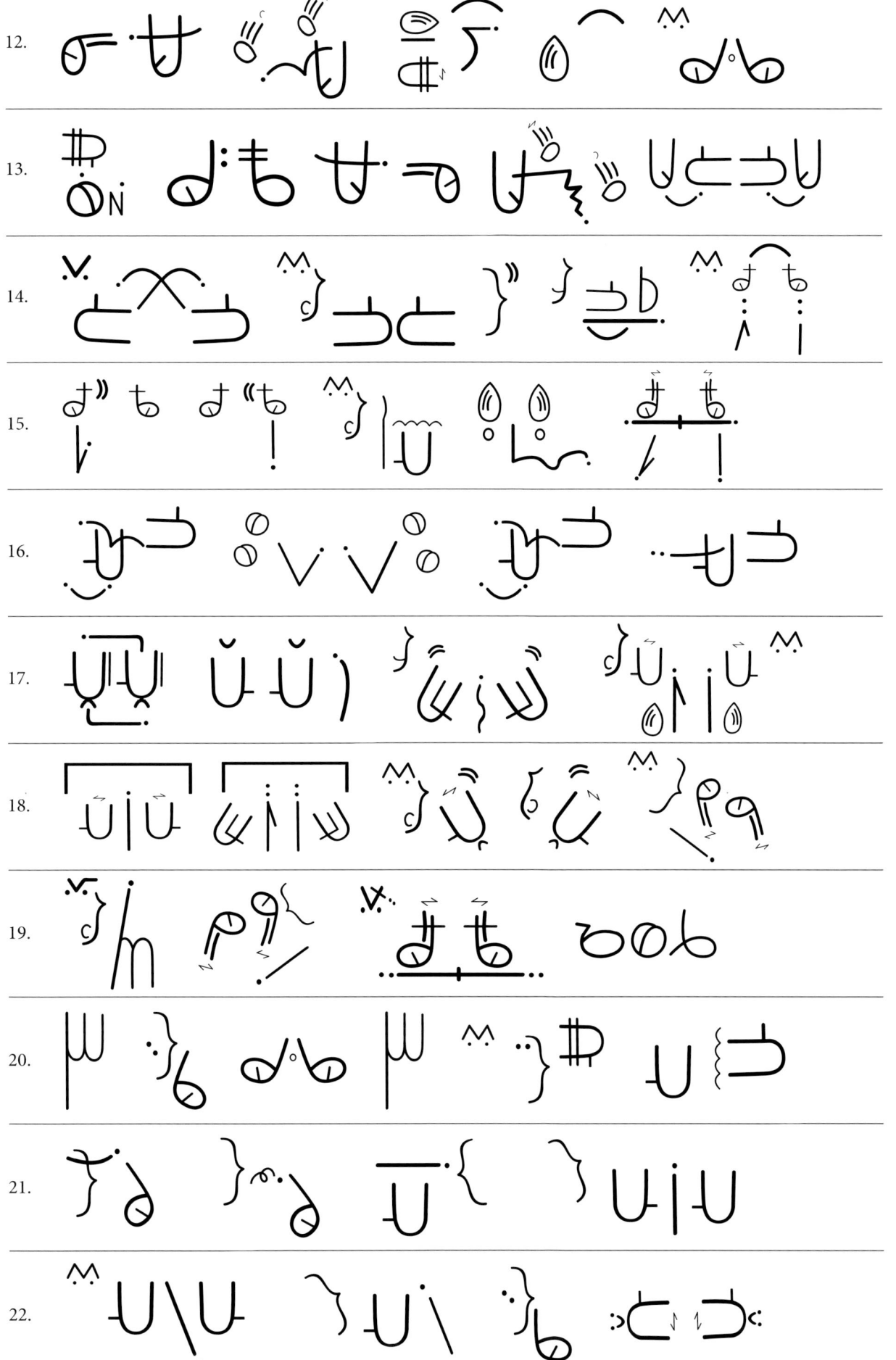

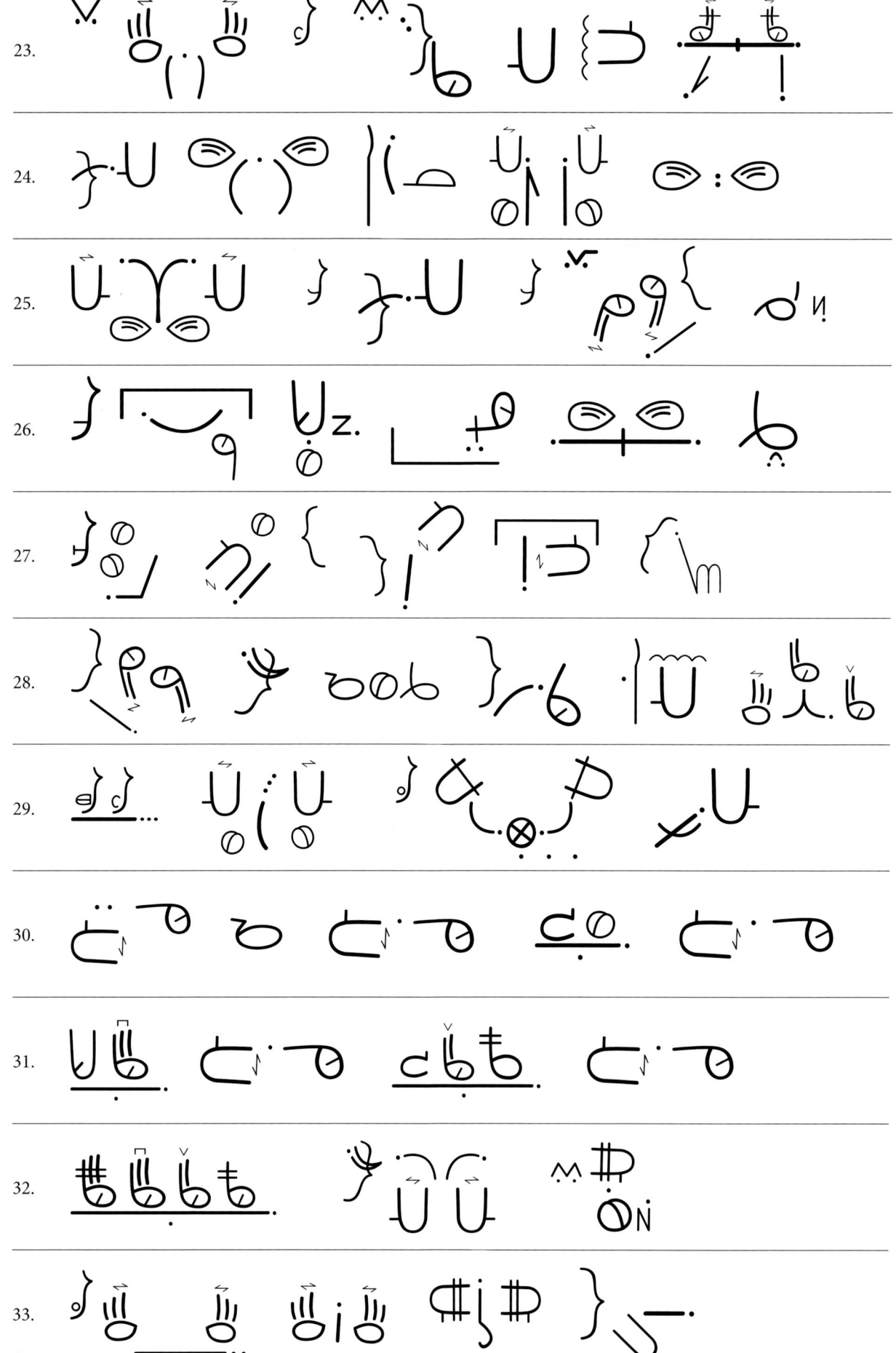

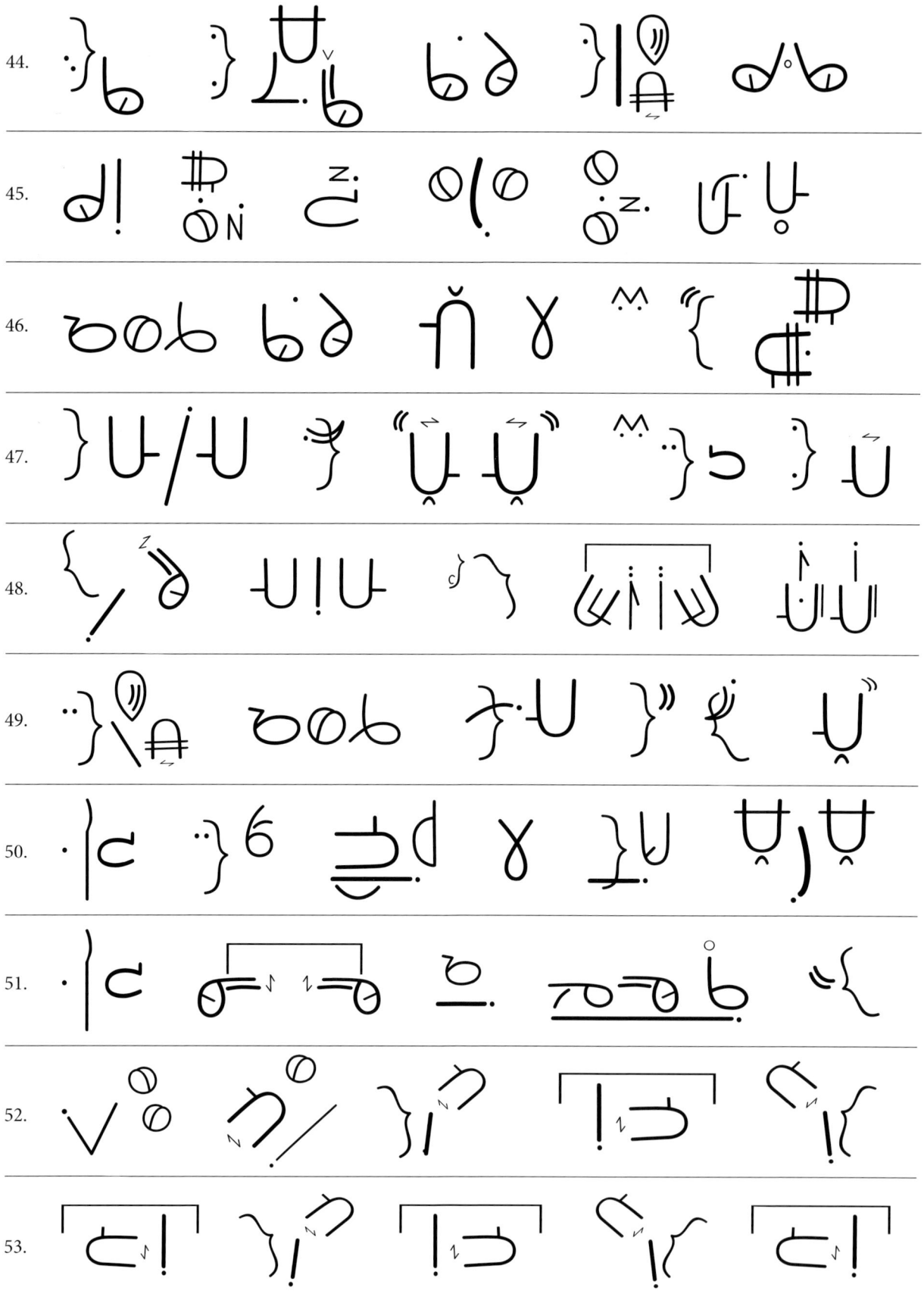

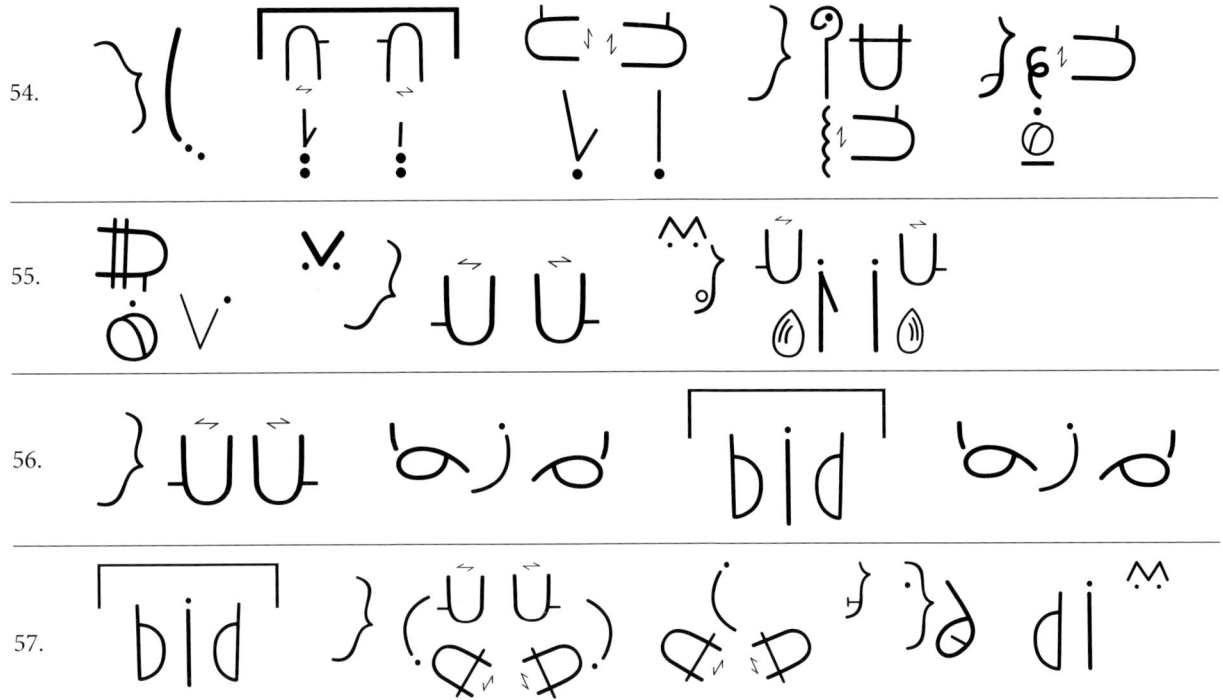

Glossary

Alternating Mark: A mark, resembling a half arrow tip, that tells which handshape moves first in a sign.

Bar, or edge, diacritic: 1.) A line mark to indicate one or more bent fingers at the upper finger joint, and 2.) A short line mark to indicate the digit orientation and locative (body) mark contact point.

Corpus: A large or complete collection of writings.

Diacritic: A symbol placed with a digit or locative mark that refers to oscillations of the hands, body and finger; and in addition for fingers, it represents bending.

Digibet: A set of digits or handshapes in written ASL.

Digit: A symbol to represent a handshape in written ASL.

Double Bars diacritic: Two line marks to indicate one or more bent fingers at the lower finger joint.

Endpoint: One or more dots at the end of a movement line.

Flutter diacritic: A wavy line mark that indicates the alternative wiggling of two or more fingers simultaneously, but not together.

Grammar: The string of structural rules that direct the composition of words, phrases, and clauses in a natural language.

Half-square diacritic: A mark that uses one or more fingers folded to rest on a closed thumb.

Hinge diacritic: An arc mark that represents two functions: 1.) a sideways or back-and-forth digit motion, and 2.) a halfway closure where one or two fingers almost touch the thumb tip.

Indicator mark: A mark that indicates a specific function or purpose in the production of a word.

Inflection: The linguistic term for a morpheme that adds grammatical information to a word or a sign.

Layman's terms: The description of a complex or technical issue using words and terms that any individual can understand.

Linguist: A person who studies a language and its whole structure, syntax, and history of usage and culture.

Locative mark: A mark to indicate parts of the body.

Morphing: The use of various digits in succession for a word such as spelling lexicons or signing words.

Movement line: A line tracing the movement of the digit in certain ways as written.

Non-manual mark: A symbol to show body expression without the use of hands.

Open diacritic: A mark that represents openness in a handshape.

Pull diacritic: A pull diacritic represents two functions: 1.) short line mark to represent a pull direction of fingers away from the palm, and 2.) a mark that indicates a folded closure of one more fingers.

Pronunciation: In written ASL, signs are produced with the given properties added such as a diacritic, locative mark, movement line and end-point(s) and/or non-manual mark.

Rattle diacritic: A set of two short line marks that resemble quotation marks to represent an act of rattling motion, rapid to-fro motion, of the digit.

Ring diacritic: A circular symbol to indicate three functions: 1.) a rolling motion at the wrist, 2.) a closure of one or two fingers touching the thumb tip, and 3) to represent the equal rotation of two digits.

Second written language: Any language learned after one's first language, either spoken or signed language.

Sign language: A visual modal form of language that functions with the use of hands and body to communicate.

Spatial orientation: A use of space in ASL where a measure indicates a certain meaning.